Don't Call Me Sister!

By the same author

Shut Up Sarah (*Highland Books*)
Improving Your Written English (*How To Books*)
Researching for Writers (*How To Books*)

About the author

Marion Field was a school teacher for many years, but gave up her teaching career several years ago to concentrate on writing. After having many magazine articles published, she is now concentrating on book-length projects—another biography is expected soon. A member of the Society of Authors, The Society of Women Writers and Journalists and the Association of Christian Writers, Marion is happy to talk to groups about her experiences.

Her other interests include reading, acting and travelling. She is an active member of her local Anglican Church.

DON'T CALL ME SISTER!

Marion Field

Highland Books

GODALMING
SURREY

First published in 1993 by Petra Publications,
This second edition 1998 by Highland Books, 2 High
Pines, Knoll Road, Godalming, Surrey, GU7 2EP.

All Scripture quotations, unless otherwise noted, are taken from
the Authorized (or King James) Version, Crown copyright.

ISBN: 1-897913-45-1

Cover design by Martin Harris.

Author's photo by Cover Shots International Limited, London

Printed in Great Britain by Caledonian International Book Manu-
facturing Limited, Glasgow.

Author's note

Apart from Mr Taylor and the author, the names and characters of all the Brethren have been changed and do not represent any actual people alive or dead. The situations are real but the characters, apart from the author and Mr Taylor, are fictitious.

Contents

Foreword

When my sister first gave me the draft of this book to read, she said to me, "If you don't want to read it all, you must read certain chapters where I mention you."

I turned to the pages she mentioned and started to read, but soon found myself turning back to the beginning, where from the fist sentence, my attention was riveted and I read on and on and on, until I finished the whole script.

There is a saying, *"Truth is stranger than fiction,"* and this story bears this out in a remarkable way. It tells of a little girl's fears, of her dreams and her frustrations as she grew through adolescence and into adulthood, but also portrays the immense love and care with which she was surrounded. It is told with tremendous humour, but also a sadness as she recalls the years when so many families—her own in-cluded—were driven apart.

"Surely He hath borne our griefs and carried our sorrows..." Marion has proved the truth of this verse many times, and throughout this book her personal trust in the Lord Jesus Christ as her Saviour and Friend is very evident. Both my sister and I are very grateful for the solid grounding in the Word of God that we had in our upbringing, and for loving and caring parents, and my prayer now, is that through this book many will be encouraged to keep their eyes upon Jesus—*and Him alone*—that Name that is above every name; and for those who do not yet know Him, that this book may provoke a desire to do so.

This personal insight into the "Brethren" is a revealing and compulsive story; may it bring glory to God and a blessing to all who read it.

Meriel Forshaw

" In quietness and in confidence shall be your strength…"   *Isaiah 30 v. 15*

Author's Preface

Although I left the Exclusive Brethren thirty-six years ago, it is only during the last few years I have felt I could speak in public or write about some of the things in this book. The events described in chapter nine have left an indelible impression on me and others who suffered in the same way. It is sad that a group which originated with such humility and sincerity should have deteriorated in such a way.

However, I do not regret my upbringing in the Brethren. I am grateful for their sound Bible teaching, their upright moral code and the kindness they showed to me.

I hope this book may help others who have been through a similar trauma and may act as a warning to other similar groups.

Marion Field   February 1998

Chapter One

Why Can't I Wear A Uniform?

"**'Thousands missing everywhere'**
—that's what the headlines will say. And where will they be, sister?" The preacher's voice boomed in my head and his eyes glared into mine. "They will have been 'caught up together with the Lord in the air'. They are the true Church, the people of God, those who have seen the Light ... light ... light ... "

My eyes jerked open. There was no light anywhere. The 'blackout' curtain at the window saw to that. Lying in my bed, I trembled. At six years old, I wasn't only frightened of the dark. On that cold winter Sunday night in 1940 I had an even greater fear.

My parents belonged to the Exclusive Brethren and every Sunday evening at the 'Meeting', as our services were called, the preacher reminded us of what the Lord Jesus had done by dying on the Cross for us. His resurrection and the fact that He was always with us was stressed. But so, too, was the fact that one day He would return to the earth again and take back to Heaven with him, those who loved him. Like the early Church, the Brethren waited expectantly for that time.

"It might be tonight," the preachers constantly warned us. We must be ready at all times, we were reminded.

My elders might wait for this happening with enthusiasm, but the idea filled me with terror. Suppose the Lord Jesus did come in the night and took my parents away and left me behind. I knew I loved Him but, as a child, my thinking wasn't always logical and every Sunday night after hearing the preaching, I was terrified I might wake up in the morning and find my parents had disappeared.

Tonight was no exception. Cautiously lifting my head from the pillow, I strained my ears to listen for the murmur of my parents' voices from the next bedroom. But there was nothing. The silence shouted at me. My heart started to thump. Had the preacher's words come true at last? Had my parents really been whisked off to Heaven while I slept?

I sat up in bed. There was still no sound. Pushing back the bedclothes, I shivered as I climbed out of bed and felt along the walls for the door which had been left open. I had to find out. Fear had affected my breathing and my breath was coming in quick gasps.

Fumbling my way along the wall, I stopped outside my parent's bedroom and squeezed my eyes shut. Please God, let them still be there, I prayed earnestly. Please, oh please, don't take them without me. The silence was smothering me. All I could hear was the hammering of my heart. Had my fears been realised at last? I was about to burst into the room and fling myself at the bed when I heard something. The relief was so great, my legs almost gave way beneath me. It was the unmistakable sound of my father snoring. Stifling a sob of relief, I stumbled back to my own room and leapt into bed before any night monsters could catch me.

Hardly had I curled up again, when the grating wail of the air raid warning splintered the night silence into a thousand pieces. The Battle of Britain was taking place above us and few nights passed without that eerie banshee sound. I hated it. Before the siren stopped, my mother burst through the door, scooped me and the eiderdown up in her arms and hurried downstairs. She deposited me in our usual 'shelter'—a small cupboard under the stairs—and crawled in beside me.

"All right, darling?" she whispered. "There's nothing to be afraid of."

I wasn't afraid—not now. I never was when I was with either of my parents. I flung my arms round my mother's neck.

"I'm glad Jesus hasn't taken you to Heaven," I whispered. I was far more frightened of that happening than of the bombs.

"What?" She sounded puzzled.

"I don't want him to take you and leave me behind," I explained.

"Oh darling, of course he will take you as well when he comes. He wouldn't leave you behind."

"Are you sure?" I wasn't convinced.

"Of course I'm sure. You love Jesus, don't you?"

"Oh yes." I gave a sigh of relief. For the moment I believed her. I was just drifting off to sleep when the slamming of the front door woke me up again. "Where's Daddy gone?" I murmured sleepily.

"He's gone on duty. You know he's a 'firewatcher'."

"What's a 'firewatcher'?"

"He has to make sure no nasty bombs are dropped and cause fires."

I sat up, bumping my head on the sloping ceiling of the cupboard. I wasn't interested in bombs. I'd thought of something far more important.

"He wears a uniform. Why can't I wear a uniform?"

"It's not really a uniform, darling. It's only a tin hat and an armband. You're too little to wear anything like that. Go to sleep or you'll be tired in the morning."

But I was wide awake now. It seemed a good time to ask again some of those questions that bothered me. My mother couldn't claim she was 'too busy to talk about that now'. Selfishly I never thought she, too, needed her sleep.

"Judith wears a uniform. Why can't I?" Judith was my best friend and was not 'in the Meeting'.

My mother sighed. "Judith's in the Brownies. You know you can't join the Brownies."

"Why not?"

"Well … " I waited patiently. It was a question I'd asked before and I knew the answer but, even at six, it didn't make much sense to me. "The Brethren don't like us to belong to clubs."

"Why not?"

"Because …, because we belong to the best club of all. We love Jesus."

"Don't other people love Jesus then—only the Brethren?"

"Yes, yes of course they do," said my mother hurriedly. "It's time you went to sleep now. No more questions."

She kissed me while I was still mumbling, "Can't Brownies love Jesus?"

I shut my eyes knowing she wouldn't talk any more. I thought about 'The Brethren' who dominated our lives. Because I'd known nothing else, I was used to accepting the rules and regulations they laid down as normal. But this didn't prevent me from querying some of their more illogical edicts. However, I always had to accept the final 'no' and knew it was 'because the Brethren don't do that'.

Unfortunately there seemed to be so many things they didn't do and that were therefore banned to me. I fell asleep thinking about all the fun that Judith could have and I couldn't.

The next day my friend arrived at my house just before nine and, clutching our cardboard boxes containing the hideous gas masks, we set off for our school which was just round the corner from my house. The majority of the pupils were boys who were being 'crammed' for entrance to public schools. The academic standard was high and there was little time for play even at an early age. There were a few girls but we were relegated to the summer house in the garden for our lessons.

Judith, however, was 'clever' and was therefore taught with the boys where she learnt important things like Geometry and Latin, while the rest of us were given only a basic grounding in 'the three Rs'. We were, however, introduced to the delights of Greek Mythology and I wept buckets over the untimely death of Hector in the Trojan War.

Although I didn't see much of Judith during lesson times, out of school she spent more time at my house than I did at hers. I'm surprised her parents allowed this as she was always telling me how 'very peculiar' they thought my family was.

"They can't understand why you don't have a wireless," she told me that day at break time.

I knew the answer to that. "The wireless is WICKED," I told her smugly.

"Rubbish. 'Course it isn't."

"Mr Wickens says it is. He says it …, it brings the WORLD into your home."

"Well what's wrong with that?" demanded my tormentor.

I wasn't really sure what the WORLD was but I wasn't going to admit it. I was sure it was something really bad and knew I shouldn't have anything to do with it. Fortunately the bell saved me from admitting my ignorance and I returned to class wondering why 'The Brethren' always insisted we had to be so different from other people. Were we really so very special? There seemed to be an awful lot of other people around. Surely Jesus loved them just as much as he loved us.

But the fear of being expelled or 'withdrawn from', as it was called, from this tightly knit group was great and kept most of the members in line. Sitting at my desk, I only half listened to Mrs Phillips reading the story of Odysseus. My mind had meandered off at a tangent. I was thinking of my grandmother who had once suffered the ultimate penalty and been WITHDRAWN FROM. Her 'sin' was that she had dared to marry an 'outsider'.

To safeguard their 'exclusiveness', brothers and sisters were expected to marry 'inside' the Meeting. My grandmother, widowed at an early age with two teenagers to care for, had married a widower who was NOT A BROTHER. Although he was a devout Christian and a member of the 'Strict Baptists' — a group in many ways as rigid as the Exclusive Brethren — she was informed the Brethren could no longer 'walk with her' and she was 'withdrawn from'.

This meant she wouldn't be allowed to take Communion—or 'Break Bread' as the Brethren called it—and if she continued to attend the Meetings, she'd have to 'sit behind'. This was literal as on one of the chairs there was a board stating, 'Will those known in fellowship and the Breaking of Bread please sit IN FRONT of this board'. My grandmother, quite naturally, preferred to avoid this indignity and for some years worshipped with her husband in the Strict Baptist Chapel. She later returned to the fold but my step-grandfather never left the Strict Baptist. I smiled as I thought of him. With his white beard and upright carriage, he looked just like my idea of Abraham.

At supper that evening, my mother announced, "The Wickens have invited us to tea on Sunday."

My father groaned. "Do we have to go?" he asked in a resigned tone.

My mother looked harassed. "I think we should," she said. "It's very kind of them to invite us."

"Hm," muttered my father.

I crumbled the bread and tasteless margarine on my plate. We were only allowed about two ounces of butter per person per week and that didn't go very far.

"I don't want to go to the Wickens," I announced.

"It's only once," said my mother becoming even more harassed. "You know Mrs Wickens hasn't got any little girls and she's very fond of you."

I digested this along with a mouthful of scrambled dried egg. Like most other things, eggs were in very short supply. I could hardly remember what they tasted like.

"Why hasn't she got any little girls?" I demanded.

"Don't speak with your mouth full," rebuked my father.

I hurriedly swallowed and repeated my question.

"She's got two sons instead."

"Will they be there?"

"I expect so."

Robin and Ernest Wickens were very solemn young men in their early twenties. They seemed very ancient to me.

"Won't there be any other little girls?"

"I don't think so. Finish your supper, darling, and then you can play with Judith for a little while. I think I can hear her at the door now."

Sunday seemed a long way off and I forgot the 'tea' looming over me as I ran off to collect Margaret, my treasured china doll. Judith was clutching Susan, her 'baby' and soon we were deep in a game of hospitals with Margaret and Susan as our patients.

Sunday soon came. The 'Lord's Day', as it was always called, was the most important one of the week. On this day there were three 'Meetings' to which we were all expected to go. As my mother combed my long hair, I wriggled and squeaked when the comb met the tangles I'd acquired overnight. Parting my hair, she carefully tied it in two bunches.

In one of his letters to the Corinthians the Apostle Paul wrote it was 'a shame for a woman to cut her hair'. The Brethren took this seriously and all the sisters had long hair which was usually scraped back into a bun. I wore plaits to school and 'bunches' on Sunday. I was used to long hair and accepted the fact I couldn't have it short like some of my school friends.

After dressing me in my Sunday-best green woollen dress and green coat, my mother pulled on my little felt hat. As St. Paul had also decreed that women should 'have their heads covered', we always had to wear hats to the Meeting. This seemed perfectly natural to me; in the forties most women wore hats or headscarves outside the house so at that time we didn't appear so very 'different'.

The Meeting started at eleven o'clock and, as the Meeting Room was at the other end of the town and we had no car, we started early to walk through the woods. The path was well worn and I trotted happily along beside my parents, occasionally stopping to inspect an unusual shaped tree trunk or stare at a squirrel squirming up a tree.

On that December morning the sun smiled on a cold-sharp world and I felt secure and happy with the two people I loved most. When we reached the Meeting Room, we joined others going into the small plain building. The only thing that identified it as a place of worship was the board outside which read: **THE WORD OF GOD WILL BE PREACHED EVERY LORD'S DAY EVENING AT 6.30, GOD WILLING.**

The inside of the Room was austere and without orna-mentation of any kind as it was felt any decoration would detract from the worship of God. I was used to the plainness but as I followed my parents in, I felt God surely wouldn't mind a little colour as he'd made such a beautifully coloured world. It seemed such a shame we were worshipping in such drab surroundings.

The chairs were arranged in a square with four blocks of several rows each and I walked behind my parents to our usual 'row'. As we sat down, my father pushed a hassock in front of each of us. I was glad of it as my feet didn't quite reach the floor but I was never quite sure why all the sisters needed them as we never knelt for prayer in the Meeting Room. In the morning we remained seated for the whole Meeting. For the first time I wondered why we didn't kneel to pray. I knelt by my bed when I said my prayers at night and when we went out to tea, we often knelt after the meal so the brothers could pray for the coming Gospel Meeting. So why didn't we kneel in the Meeting Room? I decided this was just one more strange habit of the Brethren.

Most of the Brethren were now in their seats so I knew the Meeting would soon start. I stared solemnly at the table in the centre of the Room. It was covered with a white table cloth on which were a loaf of bread, a large glass of red liquid, which I knew was wine, and a small basket for the 'collection'. I didn't need any money because I was too young to 'Break Bread' and only those Breaking Bread put money in the basket.

My gaze left the table and wandered round the room. All was quiet and there was an air of expectancy. All the sisters, of course, wore hats and most of them, I thought, were dressed very dowdily. One or two of the younger ones had tried to brighten up their appearance by a brightly coloured hat or scarf. I could see that Erica Ollinshaw was even wearing a necklace under the coat she'd casually undone. I was filled with admiration for her daring. The Brethren didn't approve of jewellery. After all St. Paul stated sternly that a woman should not deck herself with 'gold and jewellery' and the Brethren took his words to heart. My mother had a little jewel box in which she had one or two pieces of jewellery but she never wore them to the Meeting. I loved to try them on and admire myself in the mirror.

Mr Wickens, sitting in the front row with his wife and two sons, cleared his throat and stood up; I removed my gaze from Erica's necklace and transferred it to him.

"We have with us this morning," he intoned, "our dear sister, Miss Angela Grey, who is commended to us by our Brethren in Southampton."

He then proceeded to read out her 'letter of commendation'. These were always sent with any brother or sister visiting another Meeting. Anyone who was remiss enough not to bring one would have to 'sit behind' as the Brethren safeguarded their 'exclusiveness' in this way. Only those of like mind with themselves were permitted to 'Break Bread'.

After reading the letter, Mr Wickens gave out the notices for the week.

"The Reading this afternoon will be at three fifteen in this Room. Mr Hutton will be preaching at Clandon this evening and Mr Carr from Farnham will preach here. On Monday there will be a Prayer Meeting at eight o'clock and the Reading on Thursday will at the same time. On Saturday the Brethren at Guildford invite us to a Fellowship Meeting where Mr Jeffries from Poole will minister (lead the Meetings). The afternoon Reading will be at three o'clock and the Ministry of the Word (a sermon by Mr Jeffries) at six thirty. The collection last week amounted to ten pounds, five shillings and sixpence."

He sat down and there was the usual pause while we waited for the Meeting to begin. We didn't use a prayer book and there was no order of service but the morning Meeting centred on Communion known as the 'Lord's Supper'. Only brothers could speak. The sisters, true to St. Paul's instructions, had to 'keep silent in the assembly'.

At last an elderly brother, Mr Freeman, gave out a hymn from our Hymn Book, *Hymns and Spiritual Songs for the Little Flock.* The hymns in it had originally been selected in 1856 and revised at intervals ever since. But apparently no one had ever thought of changing the title.

As we had no organ or piano, the brother who gave out the hymn usually started it. Mr Freeman had a very reedy tenor and invariably started on too high a note. He did so this time. I looked across the room and caught the eye of Beatrice Ellis who was my age. We both started to giggle. My mother nudged me but the more I tried to stop, the worse it got. I stuffed my handkerchief into my mouth as a few sisters joined Mr Freeman in his laudable attempts but by the third line Erica Ollinshaw and Jean Carter realised they were singing a duet and stopped in embarrassment. There was an awkward pause and then Mr Freeman tried again—an octave lower. This time it was the sisters who had difficulty in reaching the notes. The tempo was painfully slow and sounded more like funeral march than 'a joyful noise' but in spite of this, I was aware of the sincere spirit of praise that filled the Room.

After the hymn ended, there was another pause while we waited for someone to pray. We used no set prayers at all, not even 'The Lord's Prayer'. I was puzzled we never said this. After all hadn't Jesus himself told us to use it? We repeated it every day in our school assemblies so, like all children, I knew it off by heart but it was conspicuous by its absence in the Meeting. After what seemed a very long time to me, Mr Hutton stood up to pray. As usual he flung his head back at the beginning of every sentence. This fascinated me so much I found it difficult to listen to what he was saying. I put my hands in front of my face and hoped no one would notice I hadn't shut my eyes.

The peak of the Meeting was the actual 'Breaking of Bread'. This morning it was Mr Wickens who went to the table, gave thanks at great length and then broke the loaf in half. He replaced it on the plate and it was passed round the assembled company. Everyone took a small piece and passed it to his or her neighbour. As I was sitting between my parents, they passed it over me.

When the remains of the bread had been returned to the table, Mr Wickens gave thanks for the wine and that too was passed round, each brother and sister taking a sip. I watched, fascinated, as each one delicately sipped and, after passing it on, wiped his or her lips with handkerchief. No one made any attempt to wipe the cup itself. I was so used to this it never occurred to me the practice was rather unhygienic. After this, the collection basket went round and those who'd Broken Bread dropped in their offering. I assumed they were paying for the bread and wine they'd just had!

The Meeting continued with more hymns and long extempore prayers. An hour and a half is a very long time for a six year old to sit still and by twelve o'clock I was fidgeting. There was a large wall clock at the end of the room and I watched as the minute hand slowly crept past twelve. It seemed to take ages to reach six.

But at last it was half past twelve and general rustlings indicated the Meeting was over. I kicked the hassock under my chair and watched Erica carefully pull on her black leather gloves. Chairs scraped and murmurs grew louder as we stood up and greeted each other—sometimes 'with a holy kiss' as instructed by our mentor St. Paul. Even at that tender age I was aware of the love and care that emanated from this closely knit group of Christians. Mrs Wickens stooped down and presented a smooth cheek for me to kiss.

"Are you coming to tea with us then, Marion?"

It seemed a silly question as she knew we were but I smiled politely and said, "Yes." I remembered to add, "Thank you," before she turned away to talk to my mother.

The weather had turned colder and even the brisk walk home left me feeling chilly; I was glad to get inside the house which was warm by comparison although the only heating was a boiler in the kitchen kept alight at all times to heat the water. My father busied himself with lighting a fire in the dining room. My mother had already prepared it in the morning by laying twists of newspaper underneath fire-lighters—small pieces of something like wood. They were supposed to ignite but they didn't always oblige and I watched my father hold a sheet of newspaper in front of the fire to encourage the flame to burn. Unfortunately the only result was the scorching of the paper which he hurriedly dropped into the fireplace. A few wisps of grey smoke drifted up the chimney but no flame was visible. I loved the smell of scorched paper but it meant a longer wait before we had any heat.

Muttering to himself, my father twisted some more paper and struck a match. As he held it close, flames flared up and fortunately this time the firelighters responded, setting light to the wood above them. My father laid some more coal on the top and eventually this started to glow red.

I crept closer to curl up on the rug in front of the welcoming warmth. This was my favourite place. I loved to watch the red and blue tongues of fire lap at the chimney opening. Here I saw charging horsemen disappear into the dark tunnel; fragile castles changed shape and crumbled into ash while faces alternately smiled and glowered at me. Lost in my fantasy world, I could have gazed at the changing pattern for hours. I was always getting into trouble for daydreaming both at home and at school.

"Lunch is nearly ready. Wash your hands, please, Marion." The clatter of cutlery and my father's voice broke into my dreams and I reluctantly left the warmth of the fire to face the arctic regions of the hall and the downstairs cloakroom.

I yelped as I turned on the hot tap and the water scalded my little hands. My father rushed to help me and soon we were sitting round the table eating cold roast beef, potatoes and carrots. The day before we'd enjoyed 'Saturday's dinner' as I always called it. This was hot roast beef and Yorkshire pudding. Like most food, meat was rationed so the joint we had at the weekend had to last for the rest of the week as well. My father had an allotment where he grew our vegetables.

"I suppose I'd better go to the Reading this afternoon," he said as we were eating our suet pudding.

My mother handed him a second helping. "Don't forget we're going to the Wickens for tea," she reminded him. "I'll bring Marion round about half past four and we'll meet you there."

My father sighed. I knew he didn't really want to go out to tea. He would much rather be at home with his beloved books. At the afternoon Meeting, the Reading, the brothers discussed a particular book in the Bible. The Brethren knew the Scriptures well. My father, particularly, was very well informed although he rarely contributed in Meetings. He was fascinated by Church History, an interest he passed on to me, and consequently he had reservations about the Brethren's claim to be the sole followers of the 'Truth' as laid down by the early Church in *The Acts of the Apostles* and Paul's letters.

Later that afternoon my mother and I presented ourselves at the Wickens' house. I submitted to a hug from Mrs Wickens who took our hats and coats before shepherding us into the dining room where my father, Mr Wickens, Robin and Ernest were already sitting at the table. I eyed it speculatively. Despite the rationing, there was a chocolate cake, an iced sponge and even jam, a luxury we weren't often able to enjoy. Mr Wickens 'gave thanks' for the food at great length, his voice rising and falling. My mouth started to water and I wondered when we could start eating.

At last I was offered a plate of paper-thin bread and margarine. I took a slice politely; it was considered correct to eat the first piece plain so I had to wait for the second helping to enjoy the home-made plum jam. It was delicious. So was the chocolate cake.

"Can I have another piece?" I whispered to my mother.

"Well … " She looked slightly embarrassed but Mrs Wickens laughed and said of course I could. I smiled at her. She was a chatterbox. I often wondered how she managed to restrain herself from speaking in Meetings. She'd been a nurse but like most sisters had given up work when she married.

Although some married sisters went out to work, most stayed at home to look after their families. Their husbands were the undisputed heads of the household and their wives had to submit to male authority. In the Meetings, the sisters were expected to listen and learn but couldn't contribute. To me this was a fact of life and it never occurred to me to question the ruling.

After tea came the ritual I hated. We had to kneel down beside our chairs so the brothers could pray for the Gospel Meeting to be held in the evening. Mrs Wickens, my mother and I had to cover our heads with our napkins as we were not, of course, wearing hats at the tea table. To cover my embarrassment I pretended I was wearing a nurse's head-dress. I felt very uncomfortable as Mr Wickens, Robin and Ernest prayed for what seemed to me a very long time and I started to get pins and needles in my foot. It was very hard to concentrate on what was being said.

When Ernest had finished praying, there was an awkward pause while everyone waited for my father to follow suit. I was in an agony of embarrassment because I knew he wouldn't. I fidgeted but I daren't stand up until my elders did. After what seemed an interminable silence, my father pushed his chair back and got to his feet. The prayer meeting was over.

The Wickens had a car so we had the luxury of actually being driven to the evening Gospel Meeting. Inside the Meeting Room, the chairs had been turned round to face the lectern which stood at one end on a small raised platform. Mr Carr from Farnham, who was preaching, was already sitting in the front row.

We were early so I occupied myself in my usual way by watching as people came in. I didn't turn round as my parents had always stressed how ill-bred this was so I had to content myself with watching those in front of us. Erica was wearing a different hat, I noticed. I wished I had a new one for the evening.

There was no talking before the Meeting and promptly at six thirty Mr Carr stepped up on to the platform, arranged his Bible and Hymn Book on top of the lectern and cleared his throat.

"We will start by singing Hymn number 248, *I heard the voice of Jesus say, 'Come unto me and rest'*," he announced.

We all shuffled to our feet as he started it for us. This was one of my favourites and I sang lustily. I knew some of the words but I was only just starting to read. My mother showed me the place in her hymn book and I pretended to follow it. When it was finished, we sat down again while Mr Carr prayed. At the end his 'Amen' was echoed by all the brothers and we waited expectantly for the Bible readings to be announced. Sometimes these were very obscure passages from the Old Testament and when I was older, I lived in perpetual fear I would be shamed by not being able to find them. Often I would look surreptitiously at the contents page but we were expected to know our way round the Bible. I wholeheartedly approve of the custom in most churches of announcing the page number of the reading.

But on that Sunday evening I had no problem as my mother showed me the passage in her Authorised Version of the Bible. The verses were from St. John's Gospel and included the famous verse, 'Greater love hath no man than this, that a man lay down his life for his friends.' I listened as we were reminded that Jesus had died on the Cross for us, his friends, so that when we died, we would be able to go to Heaven to be with Him. It was a simple message and I'd heard it many times before. My mind wandered and I started to feel sleepy. I snuggled up to my mother and shut my eyes as Mr Carr droned on. He had a monotonous voice and didn't hold my attention the way some of our preachers did. I wouldn't have any nightmares after his preaching!

I was jerked awake as my mother stood up for the last hymn but I was too sleepy to sing this time. I yawned through it and was grateful that, after the Meeting, Mr Wickens kindly offered to drive us home so I was spared the long walk in the dark. In the winter I didn't usually go out to the Gospel Meeting, but today had been a special one as we had been out to tea.

Chapter Two

The Best Christmas Present

I opened my eyes wondering if it was morning and I could open the presents in the stocking I'd hung at the end of my bed the previous evening. The blackout was so thick it was always difficult to tell when it was day. I lay there thinking about Christmas. Judith had told me she'd go to her church and hear all about the baby Jesus being born in the stable because there wasn't any room for his mother in the inn. I wondered if the Brethren would have a special service. It didn't seem very likely, I thought sadly. No one had said anything about it.

I sighed and blew out my breath knowing that, if I could see it, it would be white in the cold air. There was no heating in any of the bedrooms. I burrowed beneath the blankets again. There had been no air raid the previous evening so for once I'd been able to sleep right through the night in my own bed.

Footsteps sounded outside the door and my mother came in.

"Happy Christmas, darling," she said dropping a kiss on my forehead. "Aren't you going to look in your stocking?"

She flung back the curtains and blackout to display a grey world. I shot up in bed, too excited to remember I was cold.

I'd just removed an apple from the stocking when my father came in carrying a parcel wrapped up in Christmas paper.

"This is for you, Marion," he said kissing me. "I know we usually have the big presents after lunch but we thought you might like to have this now."

I took the packet and hurriedly tore off the wrapping.

"Oh." I gave a gasp of pleasure. My first Bible. I gently touched the green leather binding.

"Look. I've written in it. Shall I read it to you?" He opened the front page. Inside was printed: 'To dear Marion with much love from Mummy and Daddy. Christmas 1940.'

On the opposite page was the picture of an inn. In the forecourt was a donkey loaded with bags. Beside it, two men dressed in Eastern clothes seemed to be having an argument.

I pointed at it. "Is that like the inn where Jesus was born, Daddy?"

"Yes, I'm sure it is."

"It's Jesus' birthday today, isn't it? Will we have a special Meeting?"

My parents looked at each other while I waited for an answer.

"Yes, it is Jesus' birthday," my father said at last. "But you see ... " He hesitated as if he didn't really know the answer.

My mother helped him out. "We remember about Jesus' birthday all the year round, darling, so we don't have to have a special Meeting for it, do we?"

"Why not?" It didn't seem a very satisfactory answer to me. "Judith says they have a Christmas tree in her church. Why don't we have one in the Meeting?"

"Because it's a pagan symbol," said my father quickly.

"What's a p—p—p—?"

"Daddy means the tree isn't really anything to do with Jesus," interrupted my mother.

"Oh." I thought about that for a moment and then remarked triumphantly, "We've got a Christmas tree downstairs in the lounge with all the presents round it."

"Why don't you look in your stocking?" suggested my father hurriedly, sensing deep water ahead.

Fortunately I was easily distracted and happily withdrew a packet of sweets, a colouring book, some crayons and a A *Tale of Peter Rabbit* by Beatrix Potter.

"You'd better get up now and we'll have breakfast and then you can go for a walk while I cook the lunch." My mother folded up the empty stocking and put it on the dressing table.

Downstairs my grandmother and Auntie Gwen, my father's mother and sister, were having a cup of tea. They'd arrived the previous day to spend Christmas with us. Dressed in a smart brown velvet dress with my hair in two bunches, I ran downstairs and into the dining room.

"Look!" I exclaimed holding out my new Bible.

"Very nice, dear," said my grandmother with a smile. "I see it's an Authorised Version."

My father looked slightly annoyed. "Of course it is. Why would she want a 'New Translation'?"

Mr Darby, who had been one of the founder members of the Brethren movement in the 1830s, had translated both Old and New Testaments from the original languages. His version, known to the Brethren as the 'New Translation', was published in 1881, the same year as the Revised Version. It was sometimes used in the Meetings but it was usually the Authorised Version that was read. The plethora of more modern versions was still in the future.

My mother joined in the debate. "Do you remember what happened at our Wedding Meeting, Vin?" she asked my father. He looked puzzled.

"My stepfather was annoyed because Mr Reynolds read from Mr Darby's translation. He said, 'That's not the Bible I know'."

"Yes. I remember that." He and my mother exchanged a smile and I knew they were remembering their wedding day. The Brethren weren't licensed for marriages so they'd been married in a Registry Office and a Meeting to bless the marriage had been held afterwards. We had a black and white ciné film that had been taken at my parents' reception in Alconbury, the spacious Kent home of my grandmother and her second husband. I loved to watch it. My mother had worn a calf length cream dress of flimsy georgette with a big-brimmed cream straw hat. She still had the dress and sometimes allowed me to dress up in it.

"Can we see the film today?" I asked.

"Not today, dear. There'll be all the presents to open and play with. Come and have your breakfast now."

After breakfast, I sat on the floor to look at my new Bible. I liked the pictures. Looking at the front one of the inn, I tried to imagine Mary and Joseph there. I shut my eyes and in imagination I heard Joseph's voice pleading for shelter for his wife. Then I was out on the hillside with the shepherds hearing the Angels sing and moving with them towards the stable where the Baby Jesus lay. I opened my eyes. How I wished there was a special Meeting to celebrate Jesus' birthday. We didn't even sing carols. There weren't any in our hymn book but I thoroughly enjoyed singing them at school. I sighed. I thought Jesus must be rather sad we didn't celebrate his birthday.

I knew some of the Brethren didn't even keep Christmas at home.

They didn't know what they were missing, I thought as, later, I tripped through the woods with my father on our customary Christmas morning walk. I thought gleefully of the presents that lay underneath the tree waiting for me and looked forward to the delicious lunch my mother was cooking for us.

During the war turkeys were practically unobtainable but we were soon sitting down to roast chicken with most of the trimmings. The grown ups indulged in wine and I was allowed to have my favourite ginger beer. Daddy actually gave me a wine glass and I sipped it as if I was drinking wine. I felt very grown up. Afterwards we sat in front of a roaring log fire and Auntie Gwen, dressed as Father Christmas, gave out the presents one by one. My father had devised an ingenious system which prevented anyone knowing which presents were for him or her. Instead of putting a name on our presents when we wrapped them up, we put a number. Then on the 'key' we put the name of the recipient beside the number. On one memorable occasion, a few years later, the 'key' was lost with resulting chaos!

The opening of presents took all afternoon. By the time the last one had been opened, we were ready for a drink and a piece of Christmas cake, made with whatever ingredients my mother had been able to buy with our ration coupons.

The following Christmas when I was seven was quite a different affair. For the first time in my young life I stayed for a few days away from my parents.

I'd noticed my mother seemed to be getting rather fat and one day while she was doing my hair, I decided to comment on this. I patted her stomach.

"You're fat, Mummy," I giggled. "My tummy's not fat like yours."

My mother stopped brushing my hair and turned me round to face her. She seemed slightly embarrassed. I looked at her, surprised.

"I've got something to tell you, Marion. How would you like to have a new baby brother or sister?"

I gave this some consideration and then announced, "Judith's got a sister. I'd like a sister to play with. Where will she come from?"

My mother laid her hand over her stomach. "She's growing in here at the moment."

I giggled. It seemed a funny place to be. "Why doesn't she come out here so I can see her?"

"She's not big enough yet." She paused. "Of course it might be a little brother not a sister."

"Oh." I lost interest. I didn't want a brother. I changed the subject. "Can I have a pram for Margaret for Christmas?"

"We'll see. Marion ... " She paused and I looked up at her, puzzled. "When the baby's born, we thought you might like to stay for a few days with Mr and Mrs Freeman. Norah might be home. You'd like that wouldn't you?"

I thought about it. Norah was my heroine. The Brethren considered her 'worldly' but to me, this nineteen year old daughter of one of the leading brothers in the Meeting was everything I wanted to be when I grew up. She sometimes came to the Meeting but I noticed that she didn't 'Break Bread'. However she still sat with her parents and not behind the board. She was always smartly dressed in bright colours with frivolous hats that barely covered her head. In the summer she even wore high-heeled open-toed sandals. Her jewellery was naturally disapproved of and I was sure that sometimes she even wore lipstick—something that was anathema to the Brethren who still held the Victorian view of 'painted women'. A little face powder sparingly applied might be acceptable but no other make up ever appeared on the face of a devout sister. Norah broke all the rules but seemed to get away with it.

"I like Norah," I told my mother.

"She likes you. I think she'd be pleased to have you stay with her for a little while. You'd like that too, wouldn't you?"

I nodded but I didn't expect my sister to be so inconsiderate at to be born at Christmas!

Christmas Day that year was on a Thursday and Norah came to collect me on the Tuesday. My mother had packed a little suitcase for me and I was clutching Margaret, my doll, and trying not to cry. Now the time had come, I didn't want to leave my parents. I clung to my mother.

"I don't want to go," I wailed. "Please let me stay. Please don't send me away."

"We're not sending you away, darling. It's just that I'll be busy with the baby for a little while so Norah will take care of you."

"We'll go and feed the ducks on the pond, shall we?" asked Norah taking my hand. "Come along. "We'll have fun. You can wear some of my necklaces," she added resorting to bribery.

"Really?" I looked up to see if she meant it.

"Really."

I sniffed. "All right. 'Bye, Mummy." I kissed her and then remembered something. "Please remember to make the baby a girl, not a boy."

"I'll try, darling," replied my mother trying to hide a smile.

I trotted off, holding Norah's hand. She carried my small suitcase and I clutched Margaret tightly. We walked down the road and round the corner where there was a small pond on which a family of ducks had taken up residence. We stopped.

"Here." Norah pulled a few crusts of bread out of her pocket. With bread rationed, there wasn't much to spare for our feathered friends. I took a piece and threw it. It floated on the water and a duck glided gracefully up, inclined its head and snapped at the morsel. I laughed happily. I liked feeding the ducks. I threw some more.

When the crusts had all disappeared, we set off again to the other end of the town where Norah lived. Her parents seemed very ancient to me. Her mother, tiny and white haired, presented a wrinkled cheek for me to kiss.

Mr Freeman, wisps of grey hair decorating his bald head, peered vaguely down at me over his glasses, cleared his throat and said, "Ah Marion, yes, yes." He then wandered off and Norah led me up the twisting stairs to a tiny bedroom.

It was so different from my room at home that suddenly I was overcome with homesickness. I gulped and Norah swiftly stooped down to put her arms round me.

"It's all right, dear. You'll see Mummy and Daddy again soon and then you'll have a new baby to play with."

"Don't want baby," I wailed. "Want Mummy." The floodgates opened and I howled.

I was half aware of footsteps on the stairs and Mrs Freeman's horrified voice at the door. But Norah was rocking me back and forth in her arms. Gradually my sobbing subsided and she laid me down on the bed.

"You have a little rest now while I put your things away. Then there's a surprise for tea."

I heard her moving round the room but my outburst had worn me out and soon I was fast asleep. When I woke, the room was dark and I couldn't remember where I was. I'd opened my mouth to howl again when I heard the door open and a light switch clicked. I blinked and rubbed my eyes.

"Tea time," announced Norah cheerfully. "Come along. Let's wash your hands and go down."

I gave a gasp of pleasure when I saw the table. In the centre was a small iced cake decorated with the single word MARION in tiny chocolate buttons.

"That's my name," I told Norah enthusiastically.

She laughed and Mrs Freeman, seated behind the silver tea pot, beamed.

"Norah made it as a surprise for you," she said.

"Oh thank you, Norah," I said giving her a hug.

She hugged me back and asked, "Would you like some milk to drink?"

Horror filled me. I hated milk. Vehemently I shook my head.

"You don't want milk? How about orange squash?"

I nodded with relief. Orange squash was my favourite but at home I usually had to drink water. Perhaps after all it would be fun staying with Norah. Orange squash and an iced cake with my name on it! But first I had to have a slice of dainty plain bread and margarine followed by a home-made scone and jam. Then, at last, I was allowed to help Norah cut the cake. It was chocolate and tasted delicious. Cakes were rare at that time and all the ingredients were rationed so it was a very kind action on Norah's part. The Brethren might not approve of her but to me she was really special.

The following day was Christmas Eve and after doing some shopping, Norah took me to the nearby park where there were swings and slides. It was quite cold but I enjoyed swinging high above the ground and kept encouraging Norah to push me higher and higher.

When I went to bed that night, my friend gave me one of her stockings to hang at the end of it.

"I expect Father Christmas will put some things in it for you," she whispered as she kissed me goodnight.

I didn't believe in Father Christmas any more but she'd been so kind I didn't like to disillusion her. She tiptoed out leaving the door open so a little light crept into the room. I closed my eyes and listened to the drone of traffic in the street outside. The Freemans lived near the town so there was more traffic than in the quiet road where I lived. But soon it died down. Night time driving was difficult with no street lighting at all and car lights were severely restricted. Any pedestrians who were foolhardy enough to be out at night carried torches but even these had to be covered so very little light was available to see the way.

It was, of course, dark in my room when I opened my eyes on Christmas day so I didn't know whether it was morning or not. But this time I knew where I was. It was warm and cosy in bed and I lay happily cocooned, hugging myself as I wondered what presents I should find in my stocking.

"Are you awake, Marion?" I heard Norah's whisper from the door.

"Yes," I whispered back.

"Oh good." She reverted to her normal voice and moved over to draw the curtains. It was obviously very early as it wasn't very light yet. She moved over to the bed and stood beaming down at me. "I've got a surprise for you."

"Is it a nice one?"

"It's the best. It's a wonderful Christmas present."

"What is it?" I sat up excitedly and she gave me a hug.

"You've got a lovely little sister. She was born at half past three yesterday afternoon."

"Oooh!" I squeaked. "Where is she? Can I see her?"

Norah laughed. "Not yet. She's still very tiny. But you'll see her soon. Your Mummy and Daddy send their love to you. Why don't you look in your stocking? You've got lots of presents."

This year all my gifts had been put in the stocking and there were so many they spilled out on to the bed which was soon littered with doll's clothes, books, hair ribbons and an assortment of toys to delight the heart of a seven year old. I unwrapped each one carefully and folded up the paper for it would have to be used again the following year. Paper was short during this time of deprivation. Selotape hadn't yet made its appearance so parcels were tied with string or ribbon and even that was saved. From an early age I was taught to be frugal. It was a lesson that has stayed with me.

I returned home the following Saturday. I couldn't wait to see my baby sister and rushed into the house, shouting, "Where is she? I want to see her."

"Sh. Sh. You'll wake her." A strange lady came down the stairs towards me. She wore a starched white apron over a blue dress and my mouth dropped open as I stared at her. What was she doing in my house? I scowled. Where was my mother? My lips started to tremble.

"I want Mummy," I mumbled.

"She's resting at the moment, dear," the strange lady said. "You can see her presently and your baby sister too."

"This is Nurse who's come to look after your Mummy for a little while," Norah explained.

"Oh." I wasn't very keen to share my new sister but perhaps it wouldn't be for long.

Nurse made Norah a cup of tea and gave me some orange squash as a treat and then she said we could see the baby. By this time I was quite overawed and tiptoed up the stairs behind Nurse to my mother's room. My mother was asleep but in a cot beside the bed, lay the tiniest scrap of humanity I'd ever seen. She looked no bigger than my doll, Margaret, I thought. As I peered at her, she opened her eyes and gurgled.

"She's talking to me," I said, thrilled.

Nurse laughed. "Would you like to hold her? Sit down on that chair and I'll give her to you."

I did as she said and she put the warm little bundle into my arms. I hugged her. What fun it would to be to have a baby sister of my very own. It would be much more fun than playing with Margaret. The baby was a real live doll.

During the next few days my new 'playmate' took precedence over everything else. But she didn't want to 'play' with me. She slept most of the time so I soon got bored and Margaret was reinstated in my affections.

My new sister was called Meriel, a pretty name I'd never heard before. My father had come across it in a boys' school story he'd once read. I think one of the boys' sisters had had the name and my father had never forgotten it. However I wasn't very pleased she had the same initial as I did and I was even less happy when my mother occasionally called me 'Meriel' by mistake. Our names might be very similar but I did think she ought to remember the name she'd given her firstborn!

Meriel grew rapidly and at six months she was a chubby, lively baby interested in everything around her. Sometimes I was allowed to hold her but she objected to this and wriggled so much that on one awful occasion I almost dropped her. My frantic grab at her skirt as she started to slide off my lap made her scream and brought my mother running to my aid. Meriel was removed and put to bed for an afternoon nap. But she hardly ever slept now and spent most of her time bouncing around in the cot that was rapidly becoming too small for her.

My parents decided she should be baptised before she grew any bigger. The Exclusive Brethren always baptised babies born into the Meeting. They called it 'household baptism' as the child was baptised in the faith of its parents. No magic property in the water washed sin away; the act was symbolic and it was expected that, in due course, the child would make its own commitment and ask to Break Bread.

My sister's baptism was fixed for the beginning of July. Baptism was always by complete immersion and as there were no facilities for this in the Meeting Room, it took place in the child's home. Sometimes a bath tub of water would be brought into the living room but my sister would be baptised in the bathroom where the bath would have been filled with tepid water.

I was very excited as I had never been to a baptism before—except my own of course but I'd been far too young to remember anything about that. The day before the event, my mother made some sandwiches and baked some cakes for the tea that would follow the Meeting.

Mr Green, the brother who was to preside at the ceremony, had been a close friend of my parents for some years and he arrived early on the Saturday to have lunch with us. I liked him as he always talked to me as an equal and didn't patronise me as some of the older brothers did.

Only a few close friends and relatives had been invited as our lounge wasn't very big and the bathroom was even smaller. It seemed to shrink even more as we all crowded in to witness the event. Fortunately I was allowed to stand on the lavatory seat so I had a good view of the proceedings. Meriel wore a clean white nightdress and seemed to be thoroughly enjoying the limelight. Mr Green, wearing the traditional dark suit, took her in his arms and she gurgled at him.

He held her over the water and as he dipped her underneath it, he announced, "I baptise you, Meriel Dorothy Field, in the name of the Father, the Son and the Holy Spirit."

My sister, suddenly realising what was happening, became outraged at this undignified treatment. As she was lifted up from the water, she screamed and followed this with a demonstration of her future athletic prowess. Legs and arms flailed in the water and poor Mr Green, trying to hold on to his slippery bundle, nearly fell in himself. Meriel wasn't the only one who was totally immersed that day!

I giggled but everyone else was too busy mopping up Mr Green to pay any attention to me. The poor man had to return home to change his soaked clothes before the Meeting could be held!

Later, in the lounge, Meriel, restored to good humour and clad in a pretty white smocked dress, looked the picture of innocence as she sat on my mother's knee. I waited hopefully for her to interrupt the prayers and readings from the Bible but for once she seemed overawed, only joining in the unaccompanied hymns in a lusty treble.

The Meeting was followed by tea and the sandwiches and cakes were passed round. That was the time I enjoyed the most and I hoped my mother wouldn't notice as I helped myself to a third cake. It was delicious.

Clearing up after all our visitors had left took some time. While my mother put Meriel to bed after her big day, my father washed up and I carefully and slowly dried up the crockery. When we'd finished, we sat on the sofa in the lounge and he read me a story. He'd just finished it when my mother came in. She looked tired and collapsed on to an armchair.

"I think it went very well, don't you?" my father asked.

"Mm." My mother looked as though she were miles away. Suddenly she said, "I wasn't baptised till I was seventeen, you know."

"What?" My father looked startled.

"I was thinking of my baptism. I remember I wore a nightdress and stood up in the bath and the brother said the words and swished me under the water. There were three of us."

"All at the same time? In the same bath?" My father started to laugh.

"Don't be silly," said my mother crossly. "Of course we were done one at a time."

"What happened after you'd all been—done?"

"We went to change and then there was a Meeting in the living room—like today. I remember someone read the passage about the Philippian jailor and all his household being baptised as Mr Green did today."

"Why weren't you baptised as a baby?"

My mother thought for a moment. "I'm not really sure. I think at that time some brothers felt it was only right to baptise adults who were already committed Christians."

"What's a 'committed Christian'?" I demanded. My parents could never have a private conversation when I was around!

"Someone who loves the Lord Jesus."

"Oh." I digested this and then asked, puzzled, "What's a Christian then?"

My parents looked helplessly at each other and then my father explained, "Some people call themselves Christians but they don't really understand what Jesus has done for them."

I found this very confusing but was too tired to continue the discussion. I curled up and shut my eyes.

"Come on. Bed for you," said my father scooping me up. "It's been a tiring day."

He carried me to my bedroom where I managed to stay awake just long enough to get undressed.

I saw very little of Norah after that Christmas when my sister was born. Later I heard she'd asked to Break Bread but the Brethren had refused to accept her because she was 'too worldly'. Among other misdemeanours she wore open-toed sandals! She never asked again. Instead, after she left school, she decided to get as far away as she could from her home and the Meeting. The war was still on and she enrolled in the Red Cross and was sent to Vienna.

There was one memorable occasion just after the war ended when she made a dramatic appearance at a Reading Meeting one Sunday afternoon. I was ten and now sometimes attended this meeting. I was delighted to see Norah come in with her parents and only just stopped myself waving to her. She was wearing a smart dark blue Red Cross uniform and I was green with envy. I looked forward to talking to her afterwards.

But I didn't have the chance. After the Meeting, I hovered on the brink of a swarm of brothers who had immediately surrounded this alien in their midst.

"What a shame you have to wear that worldly uniform," I heard Mr Wickens say.

"St. Paul instructs us to withdraw from evil," added Mr Pierce smugly.

Then followed a short pause which even I could sense was pregnant with emotion. It gave Norah time to draw enough breath to demolish her antagonists. I was filled with admiration for her daring.

"I only came this afternoon because my mother begged me to," she said through clenched teeth. "The reason I'm wearing this 'worldly uniform', as you call it, is because all my other clothes are still in Vienna. It may have escaped your notice but there's been a war in Europe and people there are starving. I've been trying in a small way to help them. I've even helped some of your Brethren," she snarled. "Have you ever sent them any food parcels? Do you even care they don't have enough to eat?"

She gave them no chance to reply but pushed her way through and ran out. I tried to follow her but by the time I reached the door she'd disappeared. It was years before I saw her again.

But her tirade bore fruit. On the following Saturday evening there was a Care Meeting. This was the Meeting to deal with finances and administration. Only brothers attended and at this particular one they decided unanimously to send some food parcels to their starving Brethren in Austria and Germany!

Chapter Three

Why Can't I
Watch A Play?

Forbidden to join any clubs or go to the cinema, I made the most of the options that *were* open to me. Encouraged by my father, I became an avid reader and devoured anything that came my way. I wept buckets over *Little Women* and its sequels, fell head over heels in love with *The Scarlet Pimpernel* and held my breath at *Sherlock Holmes'* adventures. My father also introduced me to Dickens, inducing more tears as well as laughter. I made a vow to read all the Master's novels before I was twenty, a vow which I almost kept.

Unfortunately this addiction didn't always endear me to my mother. I always became completely absorbed in anything I was reading and often conveniently failed to hear her when she called me to do the washing up or lay the table. When she finally managed to attract my attention, my reply was usually, "I'm just coming. I must finish this page."

Twenty minutes later the summons would be repeated and I would be forced to drag myself away from revolution-torn France or Jo's trials for more mundane duties. But through my reading, I gradually became aware of a wider world outside the narrow constraining one forced on me by the Brethren. I read of people who cared for others, who followed Christian teaching but also led interesting and even exciting lives. Surely they couldn't all be 'worldly' and 'beyond the pale'.

I became confused and couldn't explain myself to my parents. I felt as if two strings attached to my mind were pulling me in different directions. I knew everything the Brethren said was right—didn't I? I'd certainly been brain-washed from birth into believing they and only they were 'walking in the Light'. I'd repeatedly heard that all other Christian denominations had turned from 'the Light' and were 'walking in darkness'.

I was puzzled by this. The Brethren seemed a very small group to represent the 'true Church'. What about all those other people who said they were Christians and certainly led Christian lives? I'd recently become friendly with a girl called Rosemary at school. She went to one of the local Churches and was always talking about something called 'Crusaders'.

"What is it exactly?" I asked her at last having tried for some time to puzzle it out. "I thought crusaders were people who fought in the Middle Ages—in Jerusalem—or some-where."

"Yes I think they were but the 'Crusaders' I go to is a sort of club where we read the Bible and learn about Jesus."

"Oh." I thought about this. It seemed odd to go to a club for this. Weren't clubs worldly?

"Do you want to come with me one day?" she asked.

"Oh no, I couldn't!" I reacted in horror.

"Why not? You're a Christian, aren't you?"

Yes of course I was. But how could I explain to her I was some sort of superior Christian who was 'walking in the light'. What reason could I possibly give her for not going to her Christian 'club' and meeting other Christians?

She gave me a long hard stare and then said solemnly, "It's all right, Marion. I know the Brethren don't like their children mixing with anyone else." Then she suddenly giggled. "I heard my father tell a funny story the other day about the Brethren. Do you want to hear it?" She didn't wait long enough for me to make a decision but rushed on. "St. Peter was showing some people round Heaven and they came to a high wall. One of them asked why it was there and St. Peter said, 'Shh … the Brethren are on the other side but they don't know anyone else is here!' "

Like Queen Victoria, I was not amused. In fact I was embarrassed but when Rosemary invited me to tea the next day, I was surprised to hear myself accepting. My parents had never raised any objections to my visiting my friends' houses and they didn't on this occasion.

It was my first acquaintance with a Christian home that wasn't Brethren. Six other girls of about the same age were also present. Rosemary hadn't told me there were to be other visitors and I immediately retreated into the shell I reserved for 'outsiders'.

I was relieved Mrs Jeffries gave thanks before we had our tea but I thought her husband ought to have been there to do it. After all it wasn't 'seemly' for a woman to pray 'in public' was it? After tea we went into the drawing room and to my horror Mrs Jeffies handed out Bibles. I felt a prickly sensation at the back of my neck. What was I doing here? None of these people went to the Meeting. I shouldn't be taking part in their service—or whatever it was. But there was no escape. My hands were so stiff I could hardly hold the Bible. Then I heard Mrs Jeffries' gentle voice.

"We're reading the Acts of the Apostles, Marion. Can you find it in your Bible?"

I nodded. Why hadn't Rosemary told me that the 'Crusader Club' was being held in her house? My parents would never have agreed to my joining in. But as I listened to Mrs Jeffries talking about Pentecost and the coming of the Holy Spirit, the first seeds of doubt about the Brethren crept into my mind. She was explaining it quietly and clearly and her face was shining. Everything she said was supported from the Bible and her audience was rapt. Including me! How on earth could anyone doubt this lady was a sincere Christian? Her love for the Lord Jesus shone out in her face. Perhaps the Brethren didn't have a monopoly on the 'Light' after all!

I was so busy thinking about this I hadn't realised the Bible study had finished and everyone was looking at me. I blushed fiery red and hurriedly shut the Book. Apparently Mrs Jeffries had said something to me but I hadn't heard her. She repeated it.

"We're going to have a short time of prayer now, Marion. Each of us says a little prayer and then we close by saying the Grace together."

I didn't know what the 'Grace' was and I was absolutely horrified at the thought that she expected me to pray—aloud—IN PUBLIC. I was a budding 'sister' wasn't I? And sisters didn't pray in public. And I hadn't got my head covered. I couldn't fish out my crumpled handkerchief and put it on my head. And why weren't they kneeling? We always knelt after tea before 'prayer for the Gospel'. But we didn't kneel in the Meeting. I wondered if they knelt in church. I felt more confused than ever as I sat with my head bowed—only half listening to the prayers that were being said. None of the other girls seemed to be having any problem but no doubt they were used to it. I dreaded the awful pause that would come when it was my turn. Now I sympathised even more with my father. What could I say? I couldn't pray aloud.

The inevitable happened. The other girls had all said their pieces and were now waiting for me. Tiny hot needles of fear were pricking me all over. My mind was blank. It hadn't even occurred to me to say a prayer to ask for guidance.

The silence lengthened and then I had an inspiration and started to recite a hymn we often said in our Gospel Meetings. The fact it was inappropriate for the present gathering didn't worry me. I started in a high, squeaky voice.

"Jesus lingers still. 'Tis for you he waits,
And he's waited for you long ... "

My voice tailed off. I couldn't remember any more. Tears of frustration squeezed below my closed eyelids as the silence seemed to lengthen into eternity. Then I heard Mrs Jeffries' voice.

"That's a lovely hymn, isn't it? Thank you, Marion. Now let's close by saying the Grace together."

I was so relieved at being rescued I didn't listen to the 'Grace', so I still didn't discover what it was. I said a hasty goodbye and started to run home. But before I reached there, I slowed down. I still felt very confused. After my fiasco at public prayer, I was inclined to revert to my earlier thinking that the Brethren were always right. Then I remembered Mrs Jeffries' face as she'd talked of her Saviour and doubts seeped in again. She'd looked as though she was full of 'the Light'. I decided not to tell my parents about the evening and my doubts. I knew it would worry my mother who was always anxious we did nothing to upset the Brethren.

Rosemary didn't refer to my visit again and at school I soon had something else to think about. A new teacher, Mrs Colloff, had recently been employed to teach 'the girls'—apart from Judith whose ability entitled her to be taught with the 'clever' boys. Mrs Colloff was an inspiration and had no intention of letting her charges miss out on anything. She always read us a story at the end of the day and one cold afternoon in February she chose the story of *A Midsummer Night's Dream* from Lamb's *Tales from Shakespeare*.

I was riveted. I'd always loved fairy stories and I was there in the enchanted wood. I could see it so plainly. I had a vivid imagination and with no wireless or cinema to influence me, I relied entirely on my own interpretation of stories. I remembered my father had shown me some pictures of the Fairy Queen and Bottom in one of his books. Rushing home from school, I shouted to my startled mother, "Where's Daddy's Shakespeare book? I want to read it."

My mother, her hands covered in flour, looked up disapprovingly. "Don't shout, dear. What is it you want?"

I calmed down and tried to explain. "Daddy showed me a picture of Tit-Tit-Titia and Bottom."

"Titania and Bottom," corrected my mother, smiling. "Why do you want to look at it?"

"Mrs Colloff read us the story today," I told her enthusiastically. "Where is it? Can I get it?"

"You'll have to wait till I've finished this. I think it's on the top shelf. Go and wash your hands and then I'll get if for you. It's a lovely book. You mustn't make it dirty and remember to turn the pages over very carefully."

The book was beautiful. It had a green leather binding tooled with gold and was the complete works of Shakespeare. The print was tiny and the pages tissue thin. I was enthralled as I looked at the coloured pictures illustrating this great work. But I was puzzled.

"Why isn't it written like a story, Mummy?" I asked. 'It's all funny."

"It's not a story, exactly. It's a play."

"What's a play?"

"Well, people dress up and act out the story, so that other people can watch."

"Oh." I digested this and then suddenly daylight dawned. "You mean like when I dress up as Mary, Queen of Scots and pretend to have my head cut off."

"Well—yes—something like that."

I thought about it. The theatre, like the cinema, was, of course, completely out of bounds so I'd never seen a play or even heard one. Sometimes I envied my friends who went into raptures over pantomimes at Christmas but I had to be content with merely reading the stories. But I didn't think a pantomime was the same as a play. However, I knew all about 'dressing up'. A large history book with vivid illustrations was my inspiration and a picture of the poor hapless Queen of Scotland kneeling at the block, had left an indelible impression on me. As the blackout restrictions eased towards the end of the war, I commandeered the thick black material and draped it round my small form . Some of it served as a headdress and I was never happier than when trailing round the house on my way to execution.

When my father returned home that evening, I bombarded him with questions about plays, Shakespeare and *A Midsummer Night's Dream.*

"Can I go and see a play?" I demanded bouncing up and down.

My father, embarrassed, cleared his throat. "I'm sorry, darling, but … " He paused and I knew what was coming. "The Brethren don't approve of plays."

"Why not?"

"Well, I'm afraid they think they are—er—wicked and can make people do bad things." He didn't really sound convinced.

I wasn't either. Why, I wondered, could watching something 'make people do bad things'? I didn't want to go and chop off somebody's head because I'd been reading about the French Revolution. Besides, I reasoned, it might make them do 'good things' like *the Scarlet Pimpernel* and rescue people. I suggested this to my father. It seemed very logical to me and I was offended when he burst out laughing.

When he'd sobered down, he said, "I'm sorry darling. I know it sounds rather—well, unreasonable—but you know you can't go when the Brethren don't like you to. Besides

Mummy wouldn't like it. She'd worry and you wouldn't like that, would you?"

I sighed. I knew what he said was right but it was very frustrating. It never, however, occurred to me that the 'rules' could be broken. Never having known any other life, I always accepted the Brethren's ruling in the end, however much I might argue and resent it. Ultimately I accepted that what the Brethren said had to be right. Looking up at my father, I noticed he was looking quite sad and I jumped up to hug him.

"Never mind, Daddy," I said cheerfully. "I don't really want to go and see a silly old play."

He brightened up. "I'll read you some of Shakespeare's speeches if you like."

"Oh yes, please." I loved it when my father read to me. He spoke with such expression. When I shut my eyes, I could imagine I was in the place his voice had created.

I curled up in my usual place in front of the fire while he lovingly turned over the pages. He didn't sit down but began to read and I listened spellbound. I'm sure he'd forgotten I was there.

" ... *All the world's a stage*
And all the men and women merely players:"

It seemed a strange choice for a Exclusive Brother who'd just been telling his daughter about the 'evils' of the 'worldly' stage! But at the time it didn't strike me as incongruous. I understood little of what he was saying but that didn't matter at all. I was caught by the beauty of the words and the gentle rhythm.

He finished the speech and turning the pages, started another:

> *"The quality of mercy is not strained;*
> *It droppeth as the gentle rain from heaven*
> *Upon the place beneath:"*

We were so engrossed that when my mother came in to tell me it was bedtime, I found it quite an effort to return to the twentieth century.

The next day my father bought me an exercise book and I painstakingly copied out the most famous speeches. The fact that, apart from Portia's speech in *The Merchant of Venice*, they were all male soliloquies worried me not at all. I was so enthusiastic it took me hardly any time to learn them by heart. Soon I could be heard all over the house pleading with Shylock to show mercy, encouraging my troops at Agincourt and contemplating suicide with Hamlet.

My sister, now three, was not impressed with my new found oratory and frequently, to my annoyance, demanded my attention when I was in full flow. She had a toddler's curiosity and I had to hide my books and crayons in case she decided to decorate the pages. She'd already made her indelible mark on the pale walls of our lounge!

A few weeks later I again burst home from school with exciting news.

"Mummy, Mummy!" I shrieked as soon as I entered the house, "Mr and Mrs Phillips are going to take the whole school to see the film, *Henry V* next week."

"But darling," said my mother, emerging from the broom cupboard, "You know we don't go to the cinema."

"But it's a film, not a cinema."

No one had ever explained to me the connection!

"A cinema is where you go to see a film," explained my mother patiently.

"But every one else is going. I shall be the only one left out," I wailed, bursting into tears and rushing up the stairs.

In my bedroom I flung myself on the bed and wallowed in self pity. Why shouldn't I see the film? I drummed my heels on the bed in fury. I wanted to see *Henry V*. Mrs Colloff had said Shakespeare was the greatest playwright who'd ever lived. He'd written plays to be seen not read. If I could read the play, why couldn't I see it? What was the difference? I was beginning to think the Brethren were very illogical. But I supposed some of them would probably disapprove of even reading the play. I sat up, still sobbing, and hugged my knees.

At ten my life seemed to stretch before me in an endless succession of dreary Meetings. I gulped. I was being very wicked, I thought. Of course the Brethren always knew best and they always preached from the Bible. But I didn't remember anything in it about not being able to watch films or plays. I didn't think Jesus would mind if I went. But the Bible told us to obey our parents and they said I couldn't go so I knew I'd have to accept it. I'd never have done anything without their consent.

It was starting to get dark when my mother came into the room with Meriel tucked under her arm. She made no reference to the film.

"Will you look after her while I get tea ready? She keeps getting under my feet." She dumped her burden on the floor and I rolled off the bed just in time to stop my sister grabbing my precious book of soliloquies.

"Me write," she demanded stretching out her chubby fingers. I found a piece of paper I'd already used and a red crayon. I gave them to her and while she concentrated on her art work, I thought longingly of seeing *Henry V* brought to life on a silver screen.

A surprise was in store for me. Having sulked all through tea, I was startled when my father commented, "So you want to see *Henry V*, do you?"

"Yes I do. Everyone else is going and I'll be the only one left out."

There was a slight pause while I debated whether to continue to sulk or to smile pleadingly at him. Before I could decide, he spoke again.

"Mummy and I have discussed it and we've decided that just this once you can go. But remember we can't make a habit of it so don't expect to go again."

I couldn't believe it. It was the first time we'd ever deliberately flouted Brethren policy. Perhaps, after all, I wasn't the only one to think some of the 'rules' illogical.

"Oh thank you, thank you." I flew round the table to hug my parents. My mother was looking very solemn and I knew she was worried in case the Brethren discovered our misdemeanour. However, this seemed unlikely as I was the only 'Meeting child' at the school. For the next few days I savoured the thought of the treat in store. I even tried to read the play but gave up after the first few pages.

The outing surpassed my wildest expectations. On the Wednesday afternoon we were assembled in a crocodile and marched down to the local cinema. I pulled my grey velour hat well down over my face and hoped no Brethren 'spies' would see me. But once the film started, I forgot everything else. It excelled everything I'd ever known. I was entranced and naturally fell deeply in love with Laurence Olivier. How marvellous it was to hear his musical voice uttering those stirring words I'd been declaiming in the privacy of my bedroom.

Afterwards I walked home in a daze, not even caring if I was seen by any stray brothers or sisters. For the rest of the week I relived every moment of that glorious time and marched round the house exhorting my troops to step

"Once more in the breach, dear friends, once more;
Or close the wall up with our English dead."

However my Meeting life had to go on and the following Saturday there was a 'Fellowship Meeting' in Woking. I called these meetings 'Tea Meetings' as tea was provided between the two meetings. This one was held in the Church Hall of the town Parish Church. No doubt the Brethren would have preferred somewhere else but at that time Christ Church Hall was the only place in the town that would hold a large number of people.

We didn't often attend Fellowship Meetings in other places but it wouldn't have been politic to have been missing from our local one. The grey, cold day made me appreciate my warm woolly hat, scarf and gloves. The Meeting started at three o'clock and we were sitting in our places at a quarter to the hour. The seats were arranged in the same pattern as in the Meeting Room but the square, was, of course, larger.

I enjoyed watching the visitors come in. Some of the young sisters were dressed as fashionably as possible within the restrictions although bright colours were frowned upon. These meetings often acted as an unofficial marriage market as they provided one of the few opportunities to meet the opposite sex. During the tea break young brothers and sisters could be seen shyly chatting together. Marrying within the Meeting was obligatory and those who broke this rule were likely to be 'withdrawn from' as my grandmother had been.

The afternoon Meeting took the form of a Bible study or Reading like the one on Sunday afternoons; the difference was that a visiting brother, who was recognised as a leader, always took more part in a Fellowship Meeting. These 'leading brothers' or 'ministering brothers', as they were called, spent much of their time taking meetings in different parts of the country. Their 'ministry' was expected to follow the strict pattern laid down by the Brethren.

This particular Meeting was led by a Mr Rowse who had a very high squeaky voice which made me want to giggle. My father, however, considered him 'a good brother' so I was quite happy to listen although I understood little of what he said. It wasn't long before I returned to Agincourt and savoured again the memory of that famous voice. My day-dreams were punctured occasionally by the chink of the cups and saucers which had been placed under the chairs in preparation for the tea. Any unwary foot movements re-sulted in a rattle that could be heard all over the hall!

I was relieved when they could be put to their proper use and I was able to stand up briefly. The chairs were no more comfortable than those in the Meeting Room. Anxiously I eyed the large wooden container holding a selection of tiny sandwiches; I hoped I wouldn't accidentally pick up one filled with sandwich spread which I loathed. But all was well. Fish paste was very acceptable. Munching my third sandwich, I kept an eye on a chocolate iced bun on the cake tray. Would any one take it before it reached me? I was relieved when no one did and I followed this with a piece of rather dry fruit cake.

Then all was hustle and bustle as the tea things were collected, an army of sisters decamped to the kitchen to wash up and the brothers reorganised the furniture so all the chairs faced the stage from where Mr Rowse would address us. I gazed, intrigued, at the stage waiting for the curtains to be drawn back but when they were, I was very disappointed. I don't know what I expected to see but it certainly wasn't bare wooden boards, dirty grey walls and a single table with a green cloth bearing the lectern brought from the Meeting Room. Could this dingy place ever 'hold the vasty fields of France'? I wondered. The audience would certainly have to work overtime. I decided films must be better than plays. Sighing, I returned to the present. The evening Meeting or 'Address', as it was called, would start in about half an hour and meanwhile people were free to greet friends and stretch their legs. My grandmother came over to talk to us. Auntie

Gwen had volunteered to babysit as Meriel was too young to attend a long meeting.

The evening meeting started with a hymn and a prayer and then I found with difficulty the book of Jeremiah from which Mr Rowse had elected to read. As he started to speak, I'm ashamed to say his voice soon acted as a lullaby and I went to sleep.

The next day my friend, Judith, was coming to tea and then she would come to the Gospel meeting with us in the evening. I'd wanted her to come for a long time and at last her parents had allowed her to do so although apparently they had reservations.

"They're afraid you'll try to convert me," she said with a grin.

"What's that mean?"

"Not sure really. I think it means you'll make me think like you do about things."

"What things?"

"Oh I don't know—wirelesses and not belonging to the Guides." She had progressed from the Brownies and I was still envious. But I didn't want to be reminded of our 'differences'.

The evening was not a success. Already Judith had leanings to the logic of Science and was not in the habit of accepting anything at face value. And she had no hesitation in speaking her mind whatever might be the outcome. Neither of these traits were what the Brethren expected in their children and she produced a few shock waves.

"Why don't you have an organ?" she hissed in a loud whisper as we sat down after the first hymn. "Everyone's singing out of tune."

I glared at her. I might not be very impressed with the sound, but she had no right to question it. Her question appeared to be rhetorical and I made no attempt to answer it. Judith ignored the preacher and started to read with great concentration the preface to the hymn book. The Gospel that evening was the basic Gospel message using the text, 'Jesus Christ came into the world to save sinners'.

After the Meeting had finished, Mr Wickens, drawn like a magnet to an 'outsider', bore down upon us and, backing Judith up against a wall, demanded without any preamble, "Are you saved?"

As the preacher had spent the last half hour talking about being saved, I was surprised to hear her say, "Don't know what you mean?"

Instead of explaining, he put his hand under my chin and lifted up my face so that I had to look at him. "Marion is, aren't you, dear? Marion loves the Lord Jesus and knows what he did for her."

I squirmed with embarrassment as I muttered, "Yes."

But my friend didn't suffer from the same feeling. "What did he do?" she enquired with interest.

Mr Wickens let go of my chin and looked at her, startled. "He died on the Cross to save you from your sins. *God so loved the world that he gave his only begotten Son that whosoever believeth in him should not perish but have everlasting life.* So if you believe in him as your Saviour, you are saved."

"Oh." Judith thought about this for a moment and then she stared up at him thoughtfully and said politely, "No I don't think I believe that, thank you. Come on Marion, your parents are waiting for us."

And, poised as ever, she grabbed hold of me and pulled me out of the room. I was mortified. I wanted her to love Jesus as I did and was quite bewildered to hear her deny the truth I had always accepted.

"Do you really believe it?" she asked me as we followed my parents down the road.

"Of course I do."

"When did you start to believe it?"

That posed a problem. I didn't know. I couldn't remember a specific time when I'd asked Jesus to come into my life. He always seemed to have been there and I often talked to him when I was playing. To me he was very real but in my mind he wasn't connected at all with all the rules and regulations that obsessed the Brethren. Judith's reaction to the standard question came as a great shock. I tried to answer her question but her mind had flitted off at a tangent.

"You know," she said shrewdly, "I don't think that man was really interested in me at all. He just asked me that like a ..., like a ritual sort of thing. He didn't expect an answer and if I'd said I was—'saved', I don't think he'd have known what to do with me." She suddenly burst out laughing and dodged past my parents to run down the road. Turning, she beckoned me. "Come on. Don't be such a slow coach."

Chapter Four

Rejected!

As I grew towards my teens, my reading changed direction. I haunted the library, which I'd been allowed to join, and became addicted to travel books. What a fascinating world I discovered. I longed to see it for myself. Would I ever be able to? Would I ever walk beneath the scorching African sun and see those fascinating grass huts? How marvellous it would be to follow in the steps of Jesus through the Holy Land! But I knew the Brethren didn't have a Meeting in either of those places and our travelling was limited to places where the Brethren met.

There were Meetings in Canada and many of my father's relatives lived there so perhaps I might be able to visit that country one day. But my relations weren't Brethren so the possibility seemed remote. Sighing, I curled up in front of the fire and, staring at the flames racing up the chimney, I let my imagination roam. I'd recently discovered Dr. Livingstone and Mary Slessor. Perhaps I could follow in their footsteps, I thought. If Mary Slessor could preach to the tribes in the wilds of Africa, why couldn't I do the same? Wasn't it time we started some Meetings in Africa? I rather fancied myself as a trail blazer. Of course there was the problem of my sex. The brothers would certainly frown on any attempt by a sister to usurp their preaching role. I shared my ambitions with my parents one night at supper.

"I think I'd like to be a missionary when I grow up," I announced.

"What?" Both my parents looked startled and I repeated my statement.

"But you can't, darling," said my mother gently. "The Brethren don't have missionaries."

I might have known! But I wasn't going to give up without a fight.

"Why not?" I demanded belligerently. "We love Jesus and the Bible tells us to, to …" I racked my brain for the appropriate scripture, " … to 'go and preach to all the nations'," I ended triumphantly.

There was an uncomfortable silence broken only by my sister throwing her spoon on the floor. My father retrieved it and then said quietly, "I'm sorry, Marion. I don't really know why we don't have missionaries. I suppose it's just one of our peculiarities." Then he remembered something. "But the early Brethren went abroad to America and Australia and, of course, Europe, where there are still Meetings."

"But we don't have any missionaries now?"

My father shook his head. "I'm afraid not."

"I want to travel," I announced baldly. "Do you think I'll ever be able to?"

"I hope so, darling," My father looked sad. Instinctively I knew my embryo wanderlust was inherited from him. But with a growing family and a widowed mother to care for, he'd never been able to fulfil his own longing to see the world. I hoped I wouldn't be so hindered and I knew he would be thrilled to travel vicariously through me.

However that was that for the moment. The vision of myself in the middle of the African jungle, surrounded by eager faces all absorbing the pearls of wisdom falling from my lips, receded. I sighed and picked up the latest copy of *Gospel Stories*, the magazine Brethren children received once a month. No other magazines entered our house and comics were strictly taboo. The Brethren naturally disapproved of them, and my father, a stickler for the proper use of English and a lover of Literature, ranked comics at the very bottom of the literary ladder.

Gospel Stories contained Bible puzzles, crosswords and quizzes, all of which helped us to learn more about the Bible. We had no Sunday Schools as children were regarded as part of 'God's family' and expected to attend as many Meetings as possible with their parents. The Bible teaching we received there was sound. Although I didn't take in all that was said, or even understand the beautiful language of the Authorised Version of the Bible, I absorbed some of it. The Gospel and the love of God was central and the general atmosphere of 'the Meeting' was loving and caring although I'd already begun to find it claustrophobic.

As well as reading, music and sport provided other outlets for me. One day my father staggered home from work under a load of gramophone records. I wasn't sure what they were at first but my mother looked annoyed. "You know the Brethren don't approve," she said crossly.

"They won't find out," retorted my father, lovingly inspecting his purchases.

"How are you going to play them?" she demanded sceptically. "We haven't got a gramophone."

My father looked sheepish. "I've ordered one," he said. "It's coming tomorrow."

"Oh, Vin, really!" But my mother couldn't stay annoyed for long and when the treasure arrived the next day, she became as enthusiastic as I was. Soon I was humming Beethoven's 'Choral Symphony' and Mendelssohn's 'Fingal's Cave', both of which have remained firm favourites. But in order to hide our secret, we had to resort to subterfuge. A large green silk tablecloth transformed our new 'toy' into an unrecognisable lump.

One winter evening we were all listening to the Masters by firelight when there was a knock at the door. Panic! Was it one of the Brethren?

"Quick. Turn it off," hissed my mother. "Where's the cover?"

"I can't find it," I gasped, frantically looking behind the sofa.

"Do hurry up!" My mother was almost dancing with impatience while my father stood helplessly by the table.

The knock came again.

"Here it is!" I exclaimed triumphantly, pushing my sister off her chair. She had decided to sit on the cover and was giggling happily at our discomfiture.

Hurriedly I flung it over the offending instrument and dashed to open the door. What an anticlimax! It was our next door neighbour!

"I'm so sorry to disturb you," he said politely, "but I wonder if I might use your 'phone. Ours is out of order."

"Oh yes—yes, of course. Come in," I invited breathlessly.

"Thank you."

Indicating the phone, I returned to the lounge to find my sister smugly clutching the green tablecloth while my father was selecting another record. Our secret was still safe!

Inspired by the Masters, I pleaded to learn the piano. Although we had no musical accompaniment in the Meetings, many Brethren possessed pianos and most young people learned to play the instrument; hymn singing round the piano on a Sunday evening was a popular pastime. My parents agreed it would be a useful accomplishment and so every Saturday morning, I took a bus to the other end of the town to be instructed in the mysteries of the piano.

Unfortunately, however, the instrument that adorned our lounge was a small organ—not a piano. Continuous pedalling and keeping one's fingers on the keyboard of this instrument was a very different technique from the light touch needed on the piano. Receiving lessons on the latter but having to practise on the former no doubt accounts for the fact that piano playing has never ranked among my accomplishments! I tried hard but it was very frustrating.

Therefore, I was delighted when a neighbour kindly offered me the use of her piano for practice. The only drawback was there was no heating in the room. Wearing woollen mittens was not conducive to brilliant piano playing and neither were the swollen chilblains which disfigured my fingers every winter.

Much as I loathed the cold weather, I often felt I could cope with it, if only I could be spared that incurable evening irritation. In the morning my fingers were often so stiff and swollen, they could hardly hold a pen. Walking wasn't always easy either and putting on my shoes was sometimes an almost impossible task. I often wondered what I'd done to be afflicted with such a miserable ailment.

I was ashamed of my hands. They were so ugly and when the chilblains burst, they looked even worse. Playing the piano was often a real struggle but I persevered. As it was cold in the practice room, at least I didn't have to suffer the irritation then. But I compensated for that when I returned to the open fire to thaw my frozen appendages. The irritation was unbearable and I could quite understand the expression, 'It drives me mad'. I'm surprised I remained sane!

My prowess at sport was not affected so much, as my favourite games were tennis and cricket which were, of course, played in the better weather. My father, an enthusiastic sportsman himself, was determined his daughters should like games as much as he did. He taught me to play both tennis and cricket at an early age. I enjoyed tennis but cricket soon became my favourite.

Of course, once again, there was no way we could join any local clubs. At this stage I didn't really miss them. As long as I could play, I didn't care who I played with or where I played. Soon I was living and breathing cricket. My father organised a cricket session every Friday evening on the local 'Green'. Some of the boys from my school and other local boys joined in while a brother from the Meeting was even occasionally seen. There were about a dozen enthusiasts every week.

I lived for Friday evenings and as I was usually the only girl, I savoured the limelight. But I was very serious about my cricket and concentrated on improving my leg sweep and off drive. I pushed to the depths of my subconscious the thought that, however good I became, I'd never be able to play for England or even for my county.

Our Friday evening gatherings could not be kept secret from the Brethren and soon my father was visited by two solemn looking brothers.

I disappeared into the garden so I wouldn't have to see them but I couldn't concentrate on anything as I was worried about what they were saying to my poor father. They didn't stay long and their visit had no effect as we continued to play but one more black mark was chalked up against my father. However he seemed to weather the storm but in me, seeds of guilt became implanted even more firmly. Why was it that anything I enjoyed was always wrong?

I'd just read Monica Baldwin's book *I Leap over the Wall*. How I sympathised with her desire to 'leap over the wall' of her cloistered nunnery and try her wings in 'the world'. Not for the first time, I glimpsed similarities between the authoritarian Roman Catholic Church and the Exclusive Brethren.

I sympathised with Monica on another level too. Having failed the eleven plus examination—twice, I managed to sail through the thirteen plus—probably because there was no intelligence test! But I found my entry to the Grammar School at the age of fourteen a real culture shock. There were so many females everywhere! The only man we ever saw was the caretaker! At the school I'd just left, I'd been practically the only girl remaining. I understood how Monica must have felt when she re-entered 'the world'.

Judith, to my regret, had moved away from Woking and taken up a scholarship to Wimbledon High School. When Mrs Colloff also left, the classes were amalgamated and all my classmates were boys. To be flung suddenly into a school of four hundred girls whose ages ranged from eleven to eighteen was unnerving. I was put into a fourth year class and, as everyone was already 'paired up', I felt like the proverbial fish out of water.

I retreated into my shell and tried to understand the intricacies of the Science and Mathematics I'd never been taught. I went to the Latin class but the teacher, discovering I'd never done any, very properly disposed of me. My feeling of inferiority to all the clever beings around me, deepened. Eventually my kind form teacher took me aside to ask me why I was so unhappy. I was startled.

"I'm not unhappy," I explained. "It's just … "

"Yes?"

I found it embarrassing to explain. "I'm not used to so many girls," I blurted out. "And they all know each other so I don't have any friends. And they all know so much."

She ignored my last sentence. "You know Beatrice Ellis and Susan Brown, don't you?"

They were both 'in the Meeting'.

"Yes. But … "

"I'll have a word with them," she said briskly gathering up her books. She gave me no chance to say anything more about my apparent lack of knowledge about anything. I cringed at the thought of her 'having a word' with Beatrice and Susan but fortunately they didn't seem to mind and for the next two terms I hovered on the fringe of their 'clique'.

Then, with the advent of Summer, I came into my own. The school had a cricket team! While banned from joining 'worldly' clubs, my parents didn't consider school clubs were in the same category. I had no difficulty getting into the cricket team where I was soon opening the batting.

After playing on equal terms with boys for years, I wasn't very impressed with 'girls' cricket'. But it finally broke down the barriers between me and my classmates. No one in the fourth year had ever before been a member of the school cricket team. I was given due recognition as my friends basked in reflected glory.

The following year my popularity again soared as I was picked for the school tennis team as well. Nearly every Saturday I would pack the necessary gear and trundle off to the station if the match was 'away' or to the school if it was 'at home'. Our energy was restored after the match by cups of tea and biscuits while we made polite conversation to our opponents. I would have preferred orange squash. I never believed that tea was more thirst quenching. It certainly never worked for me and on arrival home, I would always gulp down a much needed glass of orange squash.

Having been at last accepted by my peers, I started to enjoy school although I was still struggling to catch up academically. A detailed knowledge of Greek Mythology didn't help me to understand Geometry and while my French was above average, I'd done no Science at all.

As well as playing games, my father also took me to watch cricket at Lords. It wasn't long before Trevor Bailey, a recent Cambridge Blue, replaced Laurence Olivier as my hero. One of my favourite matches was the 'Varsity' Match between Oxford and Cambridge. Added to the thrill of watching my favourite game, was the excitement of 'dressing up'. My childhood attempts at 'uniform' and 'period costumes' had given way to the delights of modern fashion. The 'New Look' with its flowing skirts and picture hats had now replaced the skimpy dresses and drab colours of the forties. Clothes rationing was no longer in force and we were able to buy clothes for their appearance, not only for their utilitarian quality.

In the early fifties I was becoming a young lady while my sister was still a little girl. But we were both thrilled one Saturday when our parents took us on a shopping trip to London. The 'Varsity' Match was the following Saturday so I'd be able to wear my new outfit to Lords. I'd never had a complete matching outfit before.

My sister at nine was still at the tomboy stage; clothes to her were still articles to keep her warm or to preserve the decencies. She was a very modest little girl. So choosing her dress didn't take long.

I was more fussy, but at last settled on a mustard yellow in crepe silk. The mid calf skirt was flared and white piping adorned the short sleeves and sweetheart neckline. Then I had fun in the hat department, discovering, to my delight, a plain wide brimmed straw hat in exactly the same colour as my dress. Its only decoration was a white ribbon tied into a bow at the back. I felt I'd really entered the glamour stakes.

"Can I have some high heeled court shoes?" I pleaded.

"Well ... " My mother looked dubious.

"Oh let her," exclaimed my father. "She's grown up now, isn't she?"

He looked proudly at me and I preened. I was beginning to spend far too much time admiring myself in the mirror. Vanity, I knew, was a sin. The Brethren were always telling us so. But I could never understand why they disapproved so much of sisters making themselves attractive. Why was it so wicked to wear pretty colours and fashionable clothes?

Soon I was the proud possessor of a pair of tan court shoes and—joy of joys—a matching handbag. I could hardly wait to get home to try on my finery. My ensemble was completed by a pair of white net gloves and I felt nothing could be improved. Arriving home, I rushed up to my bedroom, tore off my short sleeved cotton dress and attired myself in my new finery. Twisting round, I admired myself from every angle before floating downstairs to parade before my parents and sister.

"Very nice, dear," commented my mother.

"Yes, you look lovely," beamed my father.

I glared at my sister. She was studiously occupied in reading a book upside down. "Do you like it, Meriel?" I demanded, avid for yet more praise.

She gave me a jaundiced look. "It's all right, I suppose," she admitted grudgingly. My sister could always be relied upon to cut me down to size!

But the next day I forgot her lack of enthusiasm as I attired myself in my new finery to attend the Meeting. I'm ashamed to admit that, on that occasion, I found it hard to concentrate on what was going on.

For the next week I spent all my time dreaming of the following Saturday. Only my father and I were going to Lords on this occasion. I'd been to the 'Varsity' match the previous year but this time I felt I could really take my place with all the other glamorous ladies who, with their escorts, would promenade round the pitch during the lunch break. I was looking forward to that. I would have my handsome father as my escort.

But perhaps the Brethren were right after all in their rejection of 'worldly' pleasures. These could be very unreliable as I was soon to discover.

On Saturday morning I woke up to a gentle pattering at my window. Oh no! It couldn't be! Not today! But it was.

Hurling myself out of bed, I rushed to draw the curtains. Grey skies awash with enough rain for the whole day glowered at me.

"Oh no!" I rushed out of the room and down the stairs. "Daddy, it's raining," I wailed bursting into the dining room where my father was reading the paper.

"I'm sorry, darling. It doesn't look as though it's going to clear and the weather forecast in the paper isn't good. We'll try to find another match to go to," he consoled me.

"But I wanted to go to this one and wear my new clothes." Tears were streaming down my face. There were so few outings we could go on and it seemed very hard that one to which I had looked forward with such high anticipation should be washed out—literally.

"You mustn't get so upset." My father had obviously no idea just how much this trip had meant to me. "I'll get tickets for the M.C.C. match for next Saturday. Will that do?"

I gulped. It wouldn't but it would be churlish to say so. After all it wasn't his fault the heavens had decided to empty themselves on this particular day. I tried the imitation of a smile.

"All right, Daddy. Thank you. I'll go and get dressed."

Trailing upstairs, I reflected how much the Brethren would have disapproved of our trip. Our visits to the Mecca of cricket always resembled a clandestine raid on the larder at midnight! Why did they disapprove of everything that was 'fun'?

The reason given for the ban on all these innocent pleasures was that they were 'worldly'. The Brethren took literally St. Paul's instruction to 'come out from among them and be separate'. They were determined to 'separate' themselves from 'evil'. Unfortunately, 'evil' seemed to be present in so many things. What on earth was 'evil' about watching cricket or even playing it?

One evening I raised the subject with my father. He was fascinated by Church history and was widely read but he wasn't always happy to talk about the Brethren and their 'peculiarities'. However on this occasion he was and I started to understand much that had puzzled me.

"I know St. Paul tells us to 'separate' ourselves from 'evil'," I started, "but he really means 'evil', doesn't he? Immorality and so on."

I was slightly vague about what 'immorality' was but I gathered it was something no Christian should indulge in. Even at fifteen my knowledge of the 'facts of life' was rather hazy. My mother, like many of her generation, was too shy to talk about them so I acquired my sketchy knowledge from friends and books. However, Lady Chatterley had not yet won her famous case in the courts and in those days of censorship, novels were considerably less explicit than they are today.

'Immorality' seemed the worst of the 'sins' Paul mentioned, so it seemed logical to mention it.

My father laid aside his book. "What do you want to know exactly?" he asked.

"Well other Christians join clubs and play games so why are we different?"

"The reason goes back to the last century." He settled himself back in his chair and proceeded to enjoy giving his lecture. "You see in the nineteenth century the Church of England had gone rather far away from the way in which the early Church worshipped. Mr Darby, who was an ordained minister, by the way, and some others felt the Church had become too secular and involved in things of the world."

"But the Church of England is the state church," I objected. "Surely it can't help getting involved in other things."

My father nodded. "Yes, that's one of its weaknesses of course. Mr Darby and the others felt it had gone too far. They also objected to the idea of an ordained minister. Mr Darby actually wrote a pamphlet on the 'Notion of a Clergyman'. I've got it somewhere. You might like to read it sometime. In it he strongly criticised the idea of the clergy because he said this inhibited the Holy Spirit because only the clergy were allowed to take part in services."

"Oh, I see." I thought about this and then asked shyly, "Do you agree with him?"

"Partly but I think he went too far. After all, for years the Vicar in a village was probably the only person who was able to read the Bible."

"I still don't understand why we have to 'separate' ourselves from the 'world', though," I said returning to the point at issue.

"The early Brethren, as they called themselves, considered the established Church had become too involved in worldly affairs and was no longer concerned with its spiritual function. So they 'withdrew' from it. And because they were determined not to make the same mistake and become—er—tainted, as it were, with the world, they adopted a rigid policy of 'separating' themselves from anything 'worldly' as they called it. As you know, we don't even vote in General Elections."

"Yes I begin to see," I said slowly. "I understood the policy of not letting anyone Break Bread unless they were really—Christian—but I didn't see why we couldn't have anything to do with anyone else. I suppose that's why we're called 'Exclusive'."

"Yes. Unfortunately there were soon arguments among the Brethren about doctrine and there have been several divisions. As you know, there are different groups of Brethren."

I nodded. "The Open Brethren have a meeting in the next road to ours don't they? Why are they called 'Open Brethren'?"

"That was the first division and it was over doctrine about the person of the Lord Jesus. It's a complicated story but basically they're called 'Open Brethren' because they allow anyone to Break Bread with them."

It was clearer to me now. But sadly this exclusivism which had seemed so right at first would eventually tear the Exclusive Brethren apart.

The seeds of future discord were already there when I entered the sixth form. I was studying A level English, History and French but we also had to take a 'General Studies' course. This I found fascinating as it encompassed a wide range of topics, one of which was 'Religion'. As well as discussing the tenets of the Christian faith, we also studied other religions and I found the discussions stimulating. None of the others in the class was in the Meeting although some of them were committed Christians who were members of other Churches and Chapels. There were also several agnostics and atheists.

One of these, Deborah, a very clever Scientist, had thought out her atheistic position very clearly.

"The Resurrection's just a myth," she announced one day. "It's completely illogical. It couldn't possibly have happened. There's no proof at all."

"There's no proof it didn't happen either," I said, my heart thumping painfully as it always did when I spoke up for my faith. "What happened to the Body if the Resurrection didn't take place? It's the only possible explanation that fits the facts that are known."

"I don't know how you can believe it," sighed Deborah. "It's so far-fetched."

"You have to have faith to believe it. Christians base their faith on the fact that Christ rose from the dead."

She remained unconvinced and I knew she would return to the attack later. She'd been brought up in a Christian home and knew her Bible well. On occasion she was quite capable of quoting it to demolish my arguments. This made me return to the Scriptures afresh to find passages to justify my faith even more convincingly.

In my heart I accepted without question the fact the Lord Jesus had risen from the dead. By faith I knew it. But justifying my belief in such an incredible event wasn't easy. I found Frank Morrison's book *Who Moved the Stone?* very helpful and recommended it to Deborah but I'm not sure whether she ever read it. However, like Frank Morrison, it seemed obvious to me that the only solution that actually fitted all the known historic facts was the one in which I believed. Nothing else could possibly account for the bewildering change in the disciples.

It was refreshing to meet others at the Christian Union meetings I occasionally attended who shared my views. It still surprised me to find that other Christians believed the same as I did and that our differences were only in the way we worshipped and the lives we led.

Carol, who attended one of the lively Anglican churches in Woking, was far better at supporting her beliefs from Scripture than I was. I never saw Beatrice or Susan at the Christian Union meetings and I have to confess I felt an element of guilt when I met to discuss the Scriptures with girls who were not 'in the Meeting'.

In spite of the rigidity of the Brethren, I had been so conditioned to regard them as the only people who were really worshipping and living 'in the Light', as they called it, that it never occurred to me not to ask to 'Break Bread'. I was just seventeen when I did so and Mr Wickens and Mr

Pierce were appointed to interview me to see if I was ready for this step.

It seemed the right thing to do but I was apprehensive. I knew the Brethren disapproved of some of the things I did and I hoped these wouldn't count against me. I also felt very inadequate whenever I was faced with questions of a spiritual nature from any 'leading brothers'. I had an overwhelming sense of my own inferiority when confronted by these 'holy' gentlemen.

I was sitting in the lounge reading Howard Spring's *My Son, My Son* while I waited for the visitation. But I couldn't concentrate. Would I be accepted? I knew I loved the Lord Jesus and, to show this, I wanted to remember Him at his Table. But I was afraid it wouldn't be as simple as that.

There was a knock at the front door and my heart started to hammer painfully against my ribs. For a moment I couldn't even breathe. I heard my mother open the door and male voices answering her greeting. My limbs felt paralysed. Then I realised I was still clutching my novel. Horrified, I was galvanised into action and looked frantically round for somewhere to hide it. The obvious place was under one of the sofa cushions. I hoped neither of my visitors would choose that particular seat.

Thrusting it hurriedly out of sight, I gulped in some reviving air as the door opened and my mother said brightly, "Mr Wickens and Mr Pierce have come to see you, dear."

"Hullo," I croaked enduring the customary handshake. For a moment they stood awkwardly in the doorway while I grinned nervously at them. Then I recalled my duties as a hostess. "Do sit down," I said hurriedly, motioning them vaguely in the direction of the furthest arm chair.

I swiftly forestalled Mr Wickens' attempt to sit at the end of the sofa where my forbidden book lay hidden, by sitting there myself. He promptly sat down next to me and Mr Pierce took the armchair. I could feel the hardness of the book underneath me. It was very uncomfortable so I gingerly sidled forward and perched on the edge of my seat trying to look confident.

There was a pause while we stared at each other. I could feel my face starting to go red as it always did when I was embarrassed. Surely I wasn't expected to start the conversation.

At last, to my relief, Mr Wickens cleared his throat.

"So you wish to remember the Lord at His Table," he stated thoughtfully.

"Yes I do." My voice came out in a squeak.

"Why?" barked Mr Pierce.

"Well, I … " My carefully rehearsed speech sailed out of the window, and to my annoyance, I found myself shaking. My heart was thumping and I had apparently lost control of my tongue.

"Take your time," advised Mr Wickens kindly.

I took a deep breath. "I love Jesus and he did so much for me by dying on the Cross so I …, I want to remember him. It's such a small thing to do for him but he does tell us to remember him by taking the Bread and Wine, doesn't he?" I ended lamely.

"Hm." They looked at each other and I became even more nervous. There was another uncomfortable pause while they exchanged glances. I was sure they were deciding how unworthy I was.

"When did you come to know the Lord as your personal Saviour?" enquired Mr Pierce at last.

That was a question I could never answer. "I don't know," I said weakly. "I'm afraid I can't remember an actual time and place but I do know that He is my Saviour."

"And your Lord?" queried Mr Wickens sharply.

"Yes of course."

"Ah." Now they had the opening they wanted. "Do you think he'd be happy about some of the things you do?"

I felt myself tighten into a knot and a flutter of anger stirred inside me. My hands clenched in my lap.

"I'm sure the Lord wouldn't disapprove of anything I do," I said, trying to keep calm. "I never do anything without my parents' permission." My whole body was quivering and this was having an adverse effect on my voice.

"Ah." They exchanged glances again. I'd said the wrong thing.

I decided to take the initiative and throw the ball back in their court. "What 'things' do you mean?" I asked sweetly.

Mr Pierce leant forward and looked at me earnestly. "I don't think the Lord would like to see you playing tennis on the world's tennis courts," he said.

I opened my mouth to ask, "Why not?" but thought better of it.

"And you play cricket too," accused Mr Wickens.

"Yes." I wasn't going to deny it.

"With worldly boys."

My facade of calm started to crumble. "Those 'worldly' boys know we love the Lord Jesus and sometimes we're able to talk about him to them. Jesus told us to 'preach to all creatures' didn't he?" My heart was pounding. How had I found the strength to justify myself?

"But St. Paul tells us to 'come out from among them and be separate'," countered Mr Wickens triumphantly.

I thought of quoting Jesus' words. 'Be in the world but not of it.' But I knew I should be battling against a brick wall.

Mr Pierce decided the time had come for a new approach. "Do you think the Holy Spirit dwells in you?" he asked.

"Yes," I replied immediately.

"How do you know?"

"The Holy Spirit is in all those who believe in the Lord Jesus Christ. He …, He helps me to do things and …, and to withstand temptation."

I regretted my last remark as soon as it was out—not only because it sounded so pompous. I'd given them another opening.

"But he doesn't stop you wanting to play tennis and cricket," snapped Mr Pierce.

I knew when I was beaten. To my annoyance, I felt tears start to trickle down my cheeks. Mr Wickens put his hand on my shoulder.

"Dear Marion," he said kindly, "we all love you very much but we feel"—he glanced at Mr Pierce who nodded—"that it would be better for you to wait for a little while and ask to Break Bread again later. We don't feel that you are quite—er—ready."

I couldn't say anything. I just sat there with my head bowed feeling totally rejected. But even at that moment the seeds of doubt were beginning to grow. I wasn't surprised at the result of my interview but I knew I was quite ready to remember the Lord at his table. I loved him and I'd been baptised. Therefore I didn't think there was any Scriptural reason for my being refused. I knew my rejection was solely because I didn't fit into the mould which the Brethren demanded of the sisters.

I heard the front door slam and then my mother came into the room. The tears which had been a trickle, cascaded into a flood of frustration.

"They won't have me, Mummy," I cried. "They said I've got to wait."

"There, there, darling, I'm so sorry." My mother put her arms round me.

The bitterness that had been smouldering inside me, suddenly burst into flame and I disgraced myself.

"It's not fair," I screamed. "They're hypocrites. Clive and Beatrice are both Breaking Bread and I know they do things their parents don't know about and wouldn't approve of. But everyone knows I play tennis and cricket. Why should playing tennis and cricket stop me … ?" I couldn't go on.

"You mustn't say things like that," said my mother, horrified. "Please darling, try to accept it. I'm sure the Brethren know best. You can ask again soon and then I'm sure they'll have you."

My sobs stopped. I suddenly matured and for a brief moment I had a glimpse of a much wider vision than the Brethren had allowed me to see. Then my shoulders slumped. There was nothing I could do about the situation. For the moment I had to accept it. But that was all I was going to do.

"I shall never ask to Break Bread again," I said with dignity. "I know I am ready now and the Brethren have rejected me. I know they are wrong."

Chapter Five

A 'Model' Sister

My rejection by the Brethren depressed me profoundly and I found it difficult to talk to anyone about it. Who was there to talk to? My parents were as upset as I was and there was no way I could confide in Beatrice or Susan. Beatrice, particularly, was rather embarrassed by what had happened. When she'd asked to Break Bread a few months previously, there'd been no problem. But I knew that, unknown to her parents, she sometimes went with 'outsiders' to the forbidden cinema. And Clive, who'd asked at the same time and also been received with open arms, had a reputation among some of my school friends who lived near him, for bad language. In view of these two examples, my own rejection seemed very illogical to me. I felt there was a hypocrisy about the apparent double standards. But I felt guilty at admitting this even to myself.

Neither could I talk to any of my other Christian friends at school. To do so would have seemed disloyal to the Brethren and although in my heart I criticised them, I wasn't yet ready to do so to an 'outsider'. Joan, a member of the Christian Union, attended the Methodist Church and, knowing this was less formal than the Church of England, I actually contemplated worshipping there. But in the deep recesses of my heart, I knew I would never do so. Although not happy with some of the Brethren rules, my parents would have been heartbroken if I'd deserted them. And after all the Brethren were always right, weren't they?

So I continued to attend the Meeting; I still sat with my parents and not 'behind the board'. But I was not happy. I felt resentful and the seeds of doubt continued to sprout. Then I discovered my father was blaming himself for my rejection.

I was horrified. "Of course it's not your fault, Daddy," I told him. "I expect I didn't give them the right answers. You know I haven't got the 'gift of the gab' like some of them. I wish I wasn't so shy. But I'm not as bad as I used to be, am I?"

"No, of course not." But he refused to be sidetracked. "I know the Brethren don't like it because I never take part in the Meetings."

"Why don't you, Daddy?" I asked shyly.

He thought for a moment. "I think, perhaps, like you, I'm afraid of saying the wrong thing. And also they know I don't really go along with some of their—rules. They're too restricting. The Brethren have got the Truth and their doctrine is sound and Bible based but they follow the letter of the law too closely. Love doesn't always seem to be too evident these days and they often can't see the wood for the trees. And it's getting worse," he ended, so quietly that I hardly heard him.

I was puzzled. "What do you mean?"

He wouldn't elaborate but returned to the main issue, saying with a wry grin, "I taught you to play cricket and that's probably the real reason they wouldn't accept you. They could hardly 'withdraw from' me for such a flimsy reason but perhaps they're getting back at me through you."

"Oh Daddy, I'm sure that's not true. Of course it was my fault. And I love cricket. You know I do. It's quite my favourite thing."

"Yes, I know. I'm sorry I said that. Forget it."

But it was hard to forget his words and I suddenly realised he, too, was unhappy. The scales that had started to slip from my eyes with the Brethren's rejection of me, slipped a little further.

Meanwhile a black cloud of depression trailed after me, even at school. Everything seemed pointless. I couldn't even define the unhappiness I felt. It wasn't only not being allowed to Break Bread. I realise now it was partly 'adolescent blues' but the 'cult of the teenager' was still in the future; in the fifties we had to muddle through our teens as best we could, respecting our elders and bowing to authority.

Even the fact I was made a prefect and House Captain didn't jolt me out of my lethargy. But then something happened that did. One morning in Assembly the Headmistress announced that the sixth form were to organise a House Drama Festival. As House Captain, I immediately became involved and my early attempts at 'dressing up' and 'acting' Shakespeare, started to bear fruit. We had to do two scenes from two different Shakespearean plays. I was deputed to direct a scene from *Henry IV Part One* and I had a small part in a scene from *The Taming of the Shrew*. I was thrilled and threw myself wholeheartedly into rehearsals although feelings of guilt that I was participating in something so 'worldly' niggled at me. But as my father said, this was 'school' so the Brethren could hardly object. Their disapproval of any education after sixteen was still to come. Nevertheless, I hoped they wouldn't hear about it.

But one evening, strutting across the stage as Hortensio, the feeling of guilt completely sabotaged my vocal chords to the annoyance of the producer. She remarked scathingly she had difficulty in hearing me even when I wasn't giving an impression of a voiceless frog.

Blushing with embarrassment, I retrieved my voice box and croaked out my lines. I always had great difficulty in projecting my normally quiet voice to the back of our very narrow, but long, hall and habitually went home after rehearsals hoarse from shouting—quite the wrong way to use one's voice!

But I discovered I liked directing. A few months earlier I wouldn't have found the confidence to tell my peers what to do but I soon discovered that because I knew exactly what I wanted, they respected me and did as I asked. I was not completely authoritarian, however, and was quite happy to listen to their views. We were a happy group and had many giggles over Maureen's attempts to acquire a Welsh accent for her part as Owen Glendower.

The day of the festival dawned at the end of the Spring term and the directors had to introduce the plays. *Henry IV* was first and I was terrified. It was the first time I'd spoken in front of such a vast audience. The whole school was present and at the back sat the adjudicator. It was not a competition but she would comment on our efforts.

Eventually I was pushed out between the curtains. I'd learned my speech off by heart and had been practising for days. I took a deep breath and fixed my eye on the back of the hall, whispering a quick prayer that the adjudicator would hear me. The prayer was answered and my voice came out clearly and soared to the back. I hoped I would do as well when I had to act! Having delivered my speech, I tried to retreat behind the curtains; but I couldn't find the gap and for what seemed ages I panicked, trying frantically to get out of the limelight. At last Owen Glendower, already on stage, took pity on me and thrust a costumed arm through the curtains to yank me back to safety. I staggered off stage to watch my first production from the wings. I was quite pleased with it.

Then I had to change for my part in *The Taming of the Shrew'*. I had plenty of time to get so nervous I couldn't remember my lines. However, fortunately they returned to me on stage and I think I said them in the right order. Miss Rowe told me later she'd heard every word clearly. She sounded very surprised!

The adjudicator was very kind to all of us. She obviously appreciated the amount of work that had gone into the scenes.

"The girl who introduced the first scene is to be commended on learning her little speech," she said. "It made a great difference."

I nearly fell off my chair with surprise and pride. Somebody slapped me on the back and my face was in danger of being split in two by my wide grin. Some of the self confidence lost when the Brethren had rejected me was beginning to seep back. Perhaps, after all, I was good for something. The lady was also very complimentary about both our scenes.

The Summer term continued to boost my confidence. I was elected captain of both the cricket and tennis teams and at the end of the Summer term my partner and I won the doubles tournament. There were no singles games because of lack of time and space.

Meanwhile things on the Meeting front improved slightly with the arrival of a new family in the area. There were two twin boys who were my age and three younger girls. They lived in a lovely old farm house and our families soon became very friendly as they were kindred spirits. Mr Forest and my father were soon deep in discussion about Church history while Brian, Andrew and I put the world to rights and discussed our futures. Neither of them was Breaking Bread.

"I think girls should have to do National Service," announced Brian one Summer Sunday evening, lying back in a deck chair under our apple tree. "We have to do it. Why shouldn't you?"

I was startled. "What would we do?"

"Well—why couldn't you—nurse or something for two years?"

"Mm." I thought about it. At this time all young men of eighteen had to serve two years in the Forces although if they were going to University, they could postpone their National Service until they finished their course. The Brethren were usually conscientious objectors. In the first World War many of them had been imprisoned for refusing to carry arms although they were prepared to go into the front line to help the wounded or do anything else dangerous. Later, Parliament passed an Act which allowed men to go before a Tribunal to tell the Judges why they felt they couldn't carry arms. If their reasons were acceptable, they were usually put in the new Non Combatant Corps. Most of the Brethren went into this.

"You'll go into the N.C.C., won't you?" I asked Brian and Andrew.

"Why?"

"Why?" I repeated the question, startled at their response. Teenagers who queried the Brethren's rules were a new breed to me. "All the Brethren do, don't they?" I muttered.

Andrew picked up a small apple that had dropped off the tree, tossed it up and caught it.

"I don't think many of them really think about it," he said thoughtfully. "They do it automatically because all the Brethren do."

I thought of Clive who was now in the N.C.C. and had recently been posted to Hereford. Had he thought about what he was doing? Somehow I doubted it. I never had. I'd just taken it for granted that all young men in the Brethren, whether or not they were Breaking Bread, went into the N.C.C.

"But they have to go before a Tribunal and the Judges have to be convinced they're sincere," I said trying to keep the jigsaw pieces in place. Andrew and Brian usually threw them in the air and when they landed, they made a completely different shape. I found it quite stimulating.

Andrew continued to wreck my carefully completed puzzle. "The Brethren are fairly well respected, you know. So they start off with an advantage. The Judges know all about them. They know they're law abiding citizens with sincere beliefs."

"Oh." I was relieved I was a girl and didn't have to make this momentous decision. "So you won't be conscientious objectors?" I queried.

They exchanged glances and suddenly they seemed years older than I was.

"I can understand the position the Brethren take," said Andrew at last. "But I can't say that I personally have any conscience about carrying arms so it would be hypocritical if I said I did, wouldn't it?"

"Yes." I repressed a shiver. Suddenly I felt cold. "So what will you do?"

"Brian's applied for a commission in the Marines and I hope to join the Queen's Royal Surrey Regiment."

Brian looked kindly at me. "You wouldn't really like it if there were no Christians in the armed forces would you?"

"Oh—no—of course not." I'd never thought about that either. I remembered some of the stories I'd read about the War. There was no doubt God had been with many of the officers and men who'd fought and died. We could sit under an apple tree on a balmy Sunday evening discussing anything we liked because men had fought and died to preserve our freedom. Many of them must surely have been Christians.

The thought of National Service continued to exercise my mind over the next few days. I needed some more answers. I tackled my father.

"Why were you a C. O. in the War, Daddy?"

"What on earth made you think of that?"

"Andrew and Brian were talking about National Service the other day. They're not going in the N.C.C.."

"I'm not surprised. They're very thoughtful, intelligent young men."

"But you don't agree with them."

"I have every respect for their views. Everyone has to make up his own mind. In St. John's Gospel we are told that *God so loved the world that he gave his only Son that whosoever believeth in him should not perish but have everlasting life*. If God did that for man, how could I take the life of one of God's creatures?"

"Did you say that at your tribunal?"

"Yes, I did."

"And the Judge accepted that?"

"Yes, he did."

"I'm glad I'm a girl and don't have to make that decision. I think I'd find it very difficult."

"I'm glad too," said my father giving me a hug.

"Why didn't you go in the N.C.C.?"

"I was in what was called, 'a reserved occupation'. I work for London Transport, as you know, and the work I was doing was considered important enough to keep me out of the services. I became a 'firewatcher' in the evenings."

I certainly had food for a great deal of thought. I could understand very clearly why some Christians felt they couldn't take human life which was given by God. On the other hand, the idea of our armed services completely lacking any Christians was a very unpalatable thought.

However my thoughts were soon given a new direction by the arrival of the highlight of the Brethren year—three day Meetings in Central hall, Westminster. These were held in July on a Thursday, Friday and Saturday and there were three Meetings a day. Many Brethren took time off to attend but it was possible to go to the evening Meetings and the Saturday ones only. Obviously not everyone could be free for the whole three days.

Usually one of the most important brothers would be invited to lead the Meetings although the 'Addresses' in the evening might be given by different brothers. The morning and afternoon Meetings were 'Readings' with the passages to be studied chosen by the invited brother. Between the Meetings lunch and tea would be served in nearby Caxton Hall. Although the Hall seated several thousand, it was necessary to have tickets so there was a control on the numbers and no one had to be turned away.

My parents, sister and I went up on the Saturday. It was a beautiful sunny day and the occasion provided an opportunity to show off my new clothes. I was wearing a green silk dress and an off white, straw hat with a curved brim. Its colour matched the trimming on my sweetheart neckline and round my neck I had daringly clasped the single string of pearls my father had given me for my birthday. Looking at myself in the mirror before I left, I was pleased with my appearance, although I regretted the lack of lipstick all my school friends wore with their mufti outfits.

My ten year old sister looked demure in a short sleeved floral dress with a cream panama hat. It was not hard to recognise the Brethren flooding to Central Hall. Fewer women in England now wore hats so the sisters, in their variety of headgear, were conspicuous. This morning some of the creations were very glamorous and so were the flowing dresses which were far more colourful than I was used to seeing in the sober Woking Meeting. I enjoyed watching the fashion parade.

The Meeting also provided another occasion for tentative courting to start. I surreptitiously eyed the young men but I would never have found the courage to speak to any of them. Neither could I imagine myself in the role of submissive wife. The relationship between brothers and sisters in the Meeting was still, in many ways, a Victorian one. Brothers were considered to have 'authority' over the sisters who had to be 'subject' to them. This was based on the verse in Paul's first letter to the Corinthians which stated that as *the head of every man is Christ* so *the head of the woman is the man*.

Brothers were the undisputed heads of their families and their womenfolk were expected to respect their authority and always obey them. I never had any problem about this in my own home. I respected my father and was quite happy to follow his lead. But I often had reservations about other brothers in our Meeting. It often seemed to me it was those who didn't automatically command my respect who were frequently stressing the superiority of the male sex over the female. I found this irritating as it seemed to relegate sisters to the status of second class Christians. This was not, of course, intentional as Jesus, himself, had recognised the worth of his female disciples and it was the women who'd remained at the foot of the cross and were the first to see the Risen Lord.

The authority of the leading brothers had also to be accepted by both brothers and sisters and any new doctrine unearthed from individual Scriptures had to be accepted. The recognised leader of the Exclusive Brethren in the nineteen fifties was Mr James Taylor, Junior. When his father, Mr James Taylor, Senior, died, he'd passed on the mantle of leadership to his son. Sadly, however, Mr J. T. Junior did not possess the humility and spirituality of his father.

Mr Taylor, himself, was leading these particular three day Meetings and the first one on that Saturday started, as usual, with a hymn. It was a stirring sound to hear thousands of voices uplifted in praise of their Lord. After Mr Taylor had prayed, the Scripture he had chosen was read. It was chapter eleven of the first letter to the Corinthians—a great favourite of the Brethren! This chapter focuses not only on the authority of the man but St. Paul speaks at great length about the woman's hair being her 'glory' and stresses that it is *shameful to a woman to have her hair cut off*. He also suggests that *any woman praying or prophesying with her head uncovered puts her own head to shame.*

I'm afraid I didn't find the ensuing discussion very stimulating. I'd heard it all before and I was soon fidgeting. Over and over again we were reminded that sisters must not cut their hair and must wear hats when they went out.

Over lunch, I decided to ask my father about something that had puzzled me. The idea of covering the head and not cutting the hair was so familiar I hadn't before noticed the reason Paul gives for it.

"If a woman has to have long hair and cover her head when she's praying and prophesying," I said, "doesn't that suggest that sometimes she does pray or prophesy—aloud?"

My father gave this some consideration. "She might pray aloud if there weren't any men present," he suggested.

"What about prophesying? What does that mean? I thought that prophecies were things Jesus said would happen or—or—the Old Testament prophecies and the Book of Revelation and so on."

"I think perhaps that particular verse refers only to the New Testament days." He didn't sound very convinced.

"But we still pray. Why not prophesy?"

"I don't know." I never did get a satisfactory answer to that question from the Brethren and it wasn't until years later I began to understand its meaning.

The 'spiritual gifts' to which Paul refers later in his Corinthian letter were rarely mentioned by the Brethren. As my father had suggested, the Brethren's view was that the 'spiritual gifts' bestowed by the Holy Spirit—one of which had been the gift of prophecy—had been for New Testament times only and were not available for today's Church. This didn't seem to me to be supported by what the Apostle Paul actually said but who was I to disagree with our revered leaders?

The afternoon Meeting continued to look at the same chapter and I'm afraid I soon began to see elements of farce in some of the 'doctrine' that was being propounded.

"A sister can never know when she will be called upon to pray or prophesy," boomed Mr Taylor. "Therefore I suggest she should have a hat near the back door so she can put it on if she's called to speak of the Lord to the milkman or some other tradesman."

I snorted and hastily turned my giggle into a cough. I didn't hear anything else for some time. I was too busy trying to contain my mirth. We were sitting in the middle of a row in the gallery which, of course, was packed. There was no way I could beat a hasty retreat and pretend I was in urgent need of a visit to the Ladies' Room. I had to sit there shaking, a handkerchief held to my face which was gradually turning from a delicate shade of pink to the angry red of an overripe tomato. My mother nudged me reprovingly but my mirth had to take its course.

At last I managed to return to some semblance of normality. I blew my nose loudly and wiped my eyes, hoping my neighbours would think I was suffering from a sudden attack of hay fever. But worse was to come. Mr Taylor had now homed in on verse ten. *Therefore ought the woman to have authority on her head, on account of the angels.*

To my amazement, I heard this verse was, apparently, of great significance to the Brethren.

"Sisters should wear a token of authority on their heads at all times," announced our leader. We waited in suspense to hear what the 'token' was to be. "A large ribbon or bow will suffice. A sister should wear this at all times so if she can't put on a hat, she will have the 'token' of authority on her head."

Over the next few months, we were to hear the word 'token' at almost every Meeting. During one memorable Reading in Woking, an elderly, rather eccentric brother, obviously feeling sorry for the female of the species, suddenly muttered, "If J. T. said all the brothers had got to wear yellow ties, you'd have the Meeting Rooms looking like fields of daffodils!"

I was determined this was one rule I was not going to obey.

But other obedient sisters immediately fashioned bands to go round their heads or their buns. It was only 'rebels' like me who queried this strange new doctrine. Eventually, however, even I succumbed on occasion but not because I accepted the ruling. I was still 'on probation' and as I still hoped to Break Bread one day, it seemed sensible to obey the letter of the law to keep the Brethren happy.

"It's a completely man-made rule," I complained to my father. "The word 'token' doesn't even appear in the Bible and nowhere does it suggest the 'authority' is a piece of ribbon. Anyway I should have thought the angels could see our hearts so why do we need a 'token' to tell them who we are?"

"I agree with you, Marion, but sometimes you have to go along with something even if you don't fully understand it.

I think it would be a good idea for you to wear something on your head—when you—go out to tea—or meet with Brethren."

"Oh all right," I sighed. "I'll do it just for you. To show you how 'subject' I am."

I made him a curtsey and he looked startled.

"By the way," he continued after a short pause, "talking of 'subjection' ... " He paused.

"Yes?" I prompted.

"Well, er ... um, Ernest Wickens had a word with me last night at the Prayer Meeting."

"What about?" I asked, intrigued.

"Well it seems that he, er ..., was sitting behind you at the Meeting at Central Hall and he ..., er—he couldn't concentrate on the meeting because of, er ..., your necklace."

"My necklace?"

"Yes he was so 'exercised' about it that it quite distracted him from what was going on."

"Well really!" I could hardly believe what I had heard. "If he's got nothing better to do than stare at my neck for an hour and a half, he can't be very spiritual. How dare he!" I stamped my foot angrily.

"Do calm down, darling," begged my father. "I know how you feel and I feel the same but—well—in view of ... the situation at the moment, perhaps it would be better if you didn't wear your necklace to the Meeting."

I sighed. "All right, Daddy. I suppose it was rather silly. I know the Brethren don't approve of jewellery but more sisters seem to be wearing necklaces now."

"Yes but they don't all sit in front of Ernest Wickens at Central Hall," he said with a grin.

"All right. I'll be a model sister for the next few months," I promised him.

So I religiously fashioned a bow to sit on top of the bun that I now wore to go to the Meeting and wore a hat or headscarf every time I stepped outside. My necklace remained in my jewel case. But I was still determined not to ask again to Break Bread. If it was right for me to do so, the Brethren would have to speak to me.

I'd enjoyed my two years in the sixth form and decided to spend a third year doing some extra O levels. During this year I had to think about my future career. Unfortunately the choice was as limited as everything else in my restricted life. The school gave us little career guidance and even without the Meeting limitations, there seemed to be few openings for girls in the early fifties. We could teach, nurse or work in an office. That seemed to be all. I didn't want to do any of them.

I would have liked to go to University but as I hadn't taken Latin at O level I couldn't do so; all the courses that interested me required Latin as a prerequisite.

"Teachers' Training College would be the best option for you," said my Headmistress in one of her rare interviews. "I suggest you try for some of the best Colleges and then teach."

I didn't want to teach. But then I didn't want to be a nurse or a secretary either. The things that appealed to me were, of course, unthinkable. I would have liked to follow a sporting career and try to play cricket for England or tennis at Wimbledon. But I wasn't allowed to do that. Neither could I become a writer. The Brethren would certainly not have approved of a sister's name appearing in a newspaper or magazine—or even on the cover of a book! I'd always enjoyed writing stories and over the years had filled many exercise books. But I knew there was no future in it.

Teaching seemed the obvious choice and at least College life would bear some resemblance to that of a University. I was eventually accepted by Bishop Otter College in Chichester. It was a Church of England College but was happy to accept nonconformists and we were assured there would be no indoctrination! There was no Meeting in Chichester; the nearest one was in Bognor so I supposed I would go there on Sundays.

Perhaps realising I should soon be flying the nest, the Brethren decided to take action. It was a Summer evening almost two years to the day after I'd first asked to Break Bread that I received another visit from Mr Wickens and Mr Pierce.

"Do you still wish to Break Bread with us?" Mr Wickens asked me without preamble.

"Yes."

"You love the Lord and wish to remember him at his Table?"

"Yes."

They looked at each other and then Mr Wickens announced, "We will put your name forward at the Care Meeting on Saturday but I am sure there will be no problem. No doubt your father will be there and he can let you know our decision. I am sure you will be Breaking Bread with us next Sunday."

"Thank you." I shook hands with them, slightly bemused. This time they'd avoided asking controversial questions. My position was no different from the one I'd held two years previously. But now the prize was within my grasp, I was still aware that for me nothing had changed. I'd been as ready to Break Bread on the occasion of their first visit as I was on their second. They hadn't even asked me as many questions.

The Care Meeting, which was the administrative Meeting, was held once a month on a Saturday evening and, at this time, only brothers attended. Here they discussed the disposal of the 'Collection', which was only taken at the Sunday morning Meeting, invitations to brothers to preach and 'letters of commendation' for Brethren who were visiting elsewhere. It was here also that the decision was made to admit brothers and sisters to 'fellowship in the Breaking of Bread' and to 'withdraw from' those who offended against the unwritten laws.

My father didn't always attend but obviously it was essential he did so on this occasion. It was after eleven when he came home but his face showed he was pleased.

"You'll Break Bread with us tomorrow, Marion," he announced.

Both my parents were obviously delighted but I felt numb. I couldn't work up any enthusiasm. The past two years had slipped into a vacuum and although I'd now been accepted, the original rejection still rankled. Having always regarded the Brethren as 'right' even when I disagreed with them, I still knew that, by keeping me waiting, they'd made a mistake. I was puzzled as to why they'd suddenly decided I was suitable after all. I still played cricket and tennis on 'the world's tennis courts.' I'd given them the same answers to their questions. As far as I was concerned, I'd been as ready to Break Bread two years ago as I was now. However, I was relieved I shouldn't have to 'sit behind' in the Bognor Meeting.

Chapter Six

Cinderella

At last I was a real 'sister'. In spite of my reservations about the Brethren's treatment of me, the first time I Broke Bread was a moving experience. As I ate the bread and drank the wine, I thought of the time when the Lord had instituted his 'Supper' and given similar food and drink to his disciples.

It didn't even worry me the single cup wasn't wiped before it was passed on. It wasn't until I joined the Church of England, years later, that I appreciated the Anglicans' use of the 'purificator', a white napkin with which the celebrant wipes the chalice before handing it to the next communicant. But when I met with the Brethren, I accepted the ignoring of hygiene in this instance. After all, I thought, it was unlikely the disciples had wiped the 'cup' before passing it on!

The time was drawing near for me to go to College and I was slightly apprehensive at leaving home for the first time. At the end of the Summer term I spent two weeks in a local primary school as I'd decided to teach at that level. The first person I saw when I entered the building was young Master Pierce. At seven, he was a lively youngster whose antics in the Meeting often kept me amused.

He looked at me in surprise and said loudly, "Hullo, Marion. What are you doing here?"

I glanced hastily round. "Sh. I'm going to teach here till the end of term," I hissed. "You'll have to call me, 'Miss Field'."

"O.K. Goodbye, Miss Field," he shouted as he ran off. I hoped I shouldn't find anyone else who knew me. I'd forgotten that John attended this particular school.

My first experience of teaching I found completely exhausting and I was soon having doubts about my chosen profession. At primary level one was expected to teach the whole range of subjects and I discovered I knew very little about anything. I wondered what I'd been doing for the past twelve years! For a start my maths left a great deal to be desired and I wasn't too strong on geography. I only knew where a place was if I'd been there and, at that time, I hadn't been anywhere.

"I can't possibly teach," I wailed to my parents at the end of my first week. "I don't know enough. I'm all right on English and history and, of course, P.E. but I'll never be able to teach science or maths."

"Why don't you change to secondary, then?" asked my father sensibly. "Then you could specialise, couldn't you?"

I thought about it. My brain did some swift reassembling of its ill fitting jigsaw puzzle. The pieces started to fit.

"Mm," I said at last, thoughtfully. "That might be an idea. I could certainly teach English and P.E.. I feel quite happy about them. But I've already signed up to do the primary course."

"Well surely you can change it. You're already doing English and P.E as your main subjects aren't you?"

"Yes. I suppose I could ask to change." I knew it was a good idea but I was anxious enough about going to College without having to inform the authorities I'd made a mistake before I'd even started.

By the time September came, I was a bundle of nerves. I had to go to Chichester on a Monday morning. I hardly listened to the preaching on my last Sunday evening but after Mr Carr, who was preaching, had sat down, there was an unexpected pause. Usually the packing up clatter followed almost immediately. But that night it didn't. No one seemed to want to be the first to stand up and soon there was total silence. I felt very uncomfortable and kept my eyes downcast. We might not use a Prayer Book but our Meetings had their own pattern and it was disturbing to have this upset.

At last as the silence lengthened and I began to feel we should never leave, Mr Freeman stood up.

"Oh, Lord," he prayed, "We feel this pause is unusual and we are sure that Thou has some reason for it. Thou knowest that our dear sister, Marion, is to start a new life tomorrow and we pray now that Thou wilt have Thy hand over her and keep her in Thy way. We ask this in the name of the Lord Jesus Christ. Amen."

The Brethren never used 'You' to address God. It was considered too familiar and the archaic 'Thee' and 'Thou' were always used. As Mr Freeman sat down, there was a chorus of 'Amens'—from the brothers, of course! Tears pricked my eyes. It didn't take much for my emotions to surface. I was very touched at this evidence of the Brethren's concern for me. At that moment I felt very close to the Lord and the Brethren. Mr Freeman's prayer had sewn together the familiar pattern and the clatter of scraping chairs soon followed after he sat down. As I made my way to the door, I felt surrounded by the love of my brothers and sisters. My hand was shaken, my cheek kissed and kind words of encouragement deluged me. The Brethren might 'separate' themselves from 'the World' but they really did care for their own and I'd never felt this more strongly than on that last evening of 'childhood'.

Mr Wickens had given me a 'letter of commendation' to introduce me to the Brethren at Bognor and I was surprised by the warmth of his words about 'our dear sister, Miss Marion Field'. It seemed that having finally accepted me, my shortcomings were to be overlooked.

As we had no car, I had to go to Chichester by train. Although I'd sent, in advance, a large trunk filled with books and the sort of clothes I felt suitable for a 'student', I was still festooned with cases so when I finally reached Chichester, I indulged, for once, in the luxury of a taxi to take me to the College. I'd been awarded a small grant but during my two years I knew I should have to watch every penny. Rolling up the drive in my conveyance, I admired the stately grey buildings. Originally built in the nineteenth century as a men's theological College, Bishop Otter had now changed its function and in the nineteen fifties was exclusively female. At least I thought it was until I discovered we actually had one male student!

With a number of my fellow students, I queued up at the Bursar's Office to report for duty and as I turned away, I suddenly saw a familiar face.

"Welcome to Bishop Otter, Marion." It was Maureen, the Owen Glendower of our famous production of *Henry IV* She'd entered College the previous year and had been cast as my College 'mother'. I thought the idea of second year students 'mothering' the new first years was very helpful.

"Come on. You're in Chichester dormitory. It's in the main building. I'll take you ." She seized one of my cases and I followed with the other. "There's the Chapel." She pointed and as I looked, I felt proud to be part of this, one of the earliest teaching colleges to be founded. However I wasn't quite so sure when we'd puffed upstairs and Maureen threw open a door.

"Here we are."

I looked round. A long narrow corridor sliced in half two rows of identical miniature rooms.

"Here's yours."

I peered round the door she'd just opened. I wondered where all my luggage was to go. There was hardly enough room for me. There was just enough space for a very narrow divan, a desk and chair and a curtain covering a small hanging area for clothes. I edged into the room and dumped my cases on the floor. Then, climbing over them, I collapsed on the bed. Maureen squeezed herself in and sat sedately beside me.

"It's like an egg box isn't it?" my College 'mother' remarked cheerfully. "In fact that's what we call it."

It was an apt description. The thin wooden walls didn't reach the vaulted ceiling and the tiny rooms seen from above must easily resemble the compartments in an egg box. They weren't much bigger, I thought despondently. I felt home-sick already.

"It's the oldest dormitory," Maureen informed me. She added in a matter of fact tone, "It's haunted of course."

"What?"

"There's a door at the end with steps that lead down to the Chapel. On a windy night you can hear the ghost."

"Rubbish. I don't believe in ghosts."

"Wait till you hear this one."

I could feel the hairs on the back of my neck rising. "Wh-what is it?" I quavered.

"You know the College used to be a men's College. Well apparently one night two of the students fought a duel with swords in the Chapel. One of them was fatally wounded and staggered up the stairs and died at the top."

"Ugh!" I shuddered. "Were you in this dormitory last year?"

"No thank goodness. There are some horrific stories. One girl's hair turned white overnight."

Now she had reached the realms of fantasy but before I could reply, there was a clatter in the corridor outside. More students were arriving. We climbed over the cases and went to meet them. Next door a tall fair haired girl smiled shyly.

"Hullo, I'm Olive Head."

"Marion Field." We shook hands sizing each other up. For the next two years we were destined to become close friends.

"I'll leave you now to unpack. Don't forget lunch is at one o'clock and this afternoon there's a reception for all the new students."

Maureen drifted off and I started to unpack and stow things away. It wasn't easy and I could see that tidiness, not one of my virtues, would be essential if I was to keep any sort of order in this tiny cubicle.

Olive and I sailed through the Reception in a haze and the following day we met our education lecturer whose task was to organise us into teaching groups. This was when the Sword of Damocles edged closer to my unprotected head.

Miss Smith was a tall, severe looking lady with her hair scraped back in a bun and no make up. She looked as though she would have preferred to be elsewhere on that Tuesday morning as she barked out our names and choice of teaching level.

"Miss Barnes, Primary."

"Yes, Miss Smith."

"Miss Brain, Primary."

"Yes, Miss Smith."

"Miss Craddock, Secondary."

"Yes, Miss Smith."

"Miss Craig … Miss Dodds … Miss Earl … "

My moment grew ever closer and at last arrived.

"Miss Field, Primary."

"No." My voice came out in a squeak as I hastily added, "Miss Smith."

Startled, the lecturer looked up from her list and tried to focus on the offender who had dared to interrupt the proceedings.

"What?" she snapped, peering over her glasses.

Hastily I stood up although my legs bore a resemblance to sticks of spaghetti immersed in boiling water. "I'm sorry, Miss Smith," I quavered, "but I've decided to—to—change to Secondary."

"Why?"

"Well, I—er—I want to …, to specialise more."

"When did you change your mind?" Her tone sounded a fraction kinder. I could feel waves of sympathy wafting towards me from the rest of the class.

I took a deep breath. "I spent two weeks at a Primary School at the end of last term. I … I don't think I could teach everything so I, er … " My voice trailed away.

"All right, Miss—er—Field, I can't waste any more time talking to you now. See me afterwards."

I collapsed into my seat. Olive glanced sympathetically at me and I gave her a weak grin. When the rest of students had left, I found the lady much more approachable. To my surprise I even found she actually understood my reasons for a change of direction.

Later, I also discovered, to my horror, she was an 'Exclusive sister'. For a time I was afraid that if I stepped aside from the 'narrow way' insisted on by the Brethren, she would report me and I would be 'withdrawn from'. But, fortunately, I didn't have to worry. Miss Smith was an independent lady who led her own life and was certainly not interested in 'spying' on a young sister who happened to be one of her students.

However, I think we were both relieved we didn't attend the same Meeting. She went to one at Singleton. As this was a village, it was a smaller meeting than Bognor and was unapproachable by public transport on a Sunday so unless I travelled with her—a solution which I'm sure appealed to neither of us—I had no option but to go to Bognor.

College life soon settled into a routine. But it soon became clear that it fell far short of my expectations. Far from resembling my idea of University life, it was more like a very strict boarding school. The College authorities were obviously determined to take their role *in loco parentis* seriously. The doors were locked promptly every night at half past ten and woe betide any brave spirits who failed to return in time. Some enterprising souls soon found unorthodox means of entry—an unlatched window, a skylight, a fire escape. It all added to the spice of life. But on the whole I was very law abiding and we were allowed a number of late passes during the term.

It wasn't long before I fell foul of the housekeeper; she was a buxom lady whose motherly exterior was belied by a heart of stone which had no sympathy to spare for students trying to live in conditions that even a sardine would have rejected.

She was waiting for me when I returned to my room after my first English lecture. I'd overslept so hadn't had time to tidy my room before I'd rushed off to breakfast and an early lecture. My bed wasn't even made! This was the cardinal sin.

"I do not expect, Miss Field," she told me in tones that reduced me to the level of a five year old, "to find your room in this state when I inspect it tomorrow morning. You will kindly make your bed and tidy your room—now."

"But I … "

"Now," she repeated interposing her considerable bulk between me and the door. She watched me grimly as I made my bed and scrambled to find homes for the numerous items of clothing scattered around the room.

Of course I was late for my next lecture which was Education. Miss Smith stopped in mid flow to watch sardonically as, bright red with embarrassment, I sidled in to sit next to Olive who had thoughtfully kept me a place. For the rest of the week I made a real effort to keep my room tidy and, as I didn't again occur the wrath of Mrs Ide, I assumed I met even her exacting standards.

On Sunday morning I got up early and went down to breakfast leaving my colleagues still sleeping the sleep of the exhausted. It was a glorious September day with a slight breeze necessitating occasional grabs at my fashionable new hat as I walked down to the city and waited opposite the Cathedral for the Bognor bus.

I climbed upstairs on the double decker to get the best view of my adopted county. The bus was almost empty so I had a choice of seats. Sitting at the front, I opened my handbag to check I'd brought my 'letter of commendation'. Then, satisfied, I settled back to enjoy the half hour ride.

Before long, I had my first glimpse of the sea and then we were riding along beside it and all too soon I'd reached my destination. I knew no one in Bognor and was always apprehensive when meeting new people. Holding on to my hat, I walked along the promenade checking the roads opposite until I found the one I wanted. No one was around on this Sunday morning as I walked slowly along, looking for the Meeting Room. I had no difficulty in finding it as, outside, was a board similar to the one in Woking.

Pushing open the door, I went in. I was quite early but one or two people were already sitting down. They all looked up as I entered and I shyly approached a brother who was tidying the hymn books at the back of the Room. I had my 'letter' in my hand but I found it difficult to break the reverent hush that always preceded a Meeting. I cleared my throat in embarrassment.

"I'm Marion Field," I whispered. "I've just started at Bishop Otter College. I've brought a 'letter of commendation' from Woking."

"Oh I see." He took it with a smile. "Mr Wickens told us you were coming. Welcome."

"Thank you."

"My name's Earnshaw. Perhaps you'd like to come to lunch with us. You won't want to go back to Chichester after the Meeting, will you?"

"That's very kind of you. Thank you. I should love to."

I sat next to two elderly ladies who smiled warmly at me. I later discovered they were sisters—in the family sense—and had lived in Bognor all their lives. They were charming and made me feel very welcome. Surreptitiously I watched the door as the rest of the brothers and sisters trooped in. I was delighted to see the Earnshaw family consisted of a daughter about my age and two sons in their late teens or early twenties. As the Meeting proceeded, my initial feelings of apprehension dispersed as the familiar pattern took over. I hadn't met any of these people before but because we shared the same beliefs and worshipped in the same way, I felt immediately at ease. It was like coming home.

After the Meeting I was overwhelmed by the welcome I received. Everyone, it seemed, wanted to greet me and it was some time before Mr Earnshaw could introduce me to his family.

"I've invited her to lunch," he informed his wife in the tone of one who was the undoubted master of his house.

"That's nice, dear," smiled Mrs Earnshaw. "I do hope you'll be happy here. Why don't you young people go for a walk along the front while I go home and start the lunch."

So Duncan, Tony, Andrea and I wandered down to the front where Andrea promptly removed her hat. "It'll only blow off," she said sensibly. "I should take yours off too, Marion."

Unable to resist a surreptitious glance around me, I did so. It was certainly more comfortable not having to go into contortions trying to clutch it on my head.

"So how are you liking College?" asked Duncan.

"I like it so far but it's jolly hard work. What do you do?"

"We work in the family business," replied Tony. He didn't elaborate and I was too shy to ask what it was. He continued, "Except Andrea. She's a lady of leisure."

"Oh." I wasn't quite sure how to respond to that.

But Andrea laughed and seemed quite unconcerned. "I left school in July and haven't decided what to do yet. Pa doesn't agree with girls going to College. Oh—I'm sorry." She stopped, embarrassed, and then tried to improve matters. "I mean—he didn't want me to go to College. I don't think he minds generally."

Mr Earnshaw was not the only brother to consider that educating girls was not really necessary. Many brothers still held the Victorian view that 'a woman's place was in the home' and her main career was that of a wife and mother. I was relieved my father wasn't one of them!

Fortunately Mr Earnshaw showed no signs of disapproving of me and I had a very pleasant time, staying to tea and supper after the Gospel Meeting as well. By the end of the day, I felt I'd acquired a new family and was delighted when the boys offered to drive me back to College in their new sports car. Sitting squashed between them, I felt I'd really started to live as we roared up the College drive with five minutes to spare. I waved as they sped off and then turned to rush into College just as the Warden was about to lock the door.

Olive gave me a relieved grin as I clattered into the dormitory with its usual cacophony of sound.

"We were quite worried in case you didn't make it," she said. "We were making contingency plans. I was going to unlock the door for you while Jean 'kept *cave*' outside Dr. Ward's door."

"That was thoughtful of you," I said, touched.

"Did you have a nice day?"

"I had a marvellous time," I replied enthusiastically and launched into a detailed account.

"You are lucky," she sighed when I'd finished. "College is really boring on a Sunday. There's nothing to do."

But my friends were able to turn the tables on me the following Saturday when the first College dance was held. Dancing, of course, was completely taboo for any Brethren. Many of the girls had boy friends who came down for the weekend and stayed in the town. But the College itself invited young airmen from the RAF station at nearby Tangmere and students from King Alfred's College at Winchester.

I have to admit the green eyed goddess was perched on my shoulder that evening as I watched Olive and Jean, who had the rooms on either side of mine, transform themselves from harassed students into glamorous femmes fatales. Olive wore an off the shoulder taffeta dress in lime green which swirled round her ankles. The colour accentuated her fairness and grey eyes. She looked lovely. How I envied her! Jean, who was dark, was sophisticated in black.

"I'm so sorry you can't come, Marion," said Olive as they prepared to sail off to meet their prospective *beaus*.

"So am I," I sighed. "But have a lovely time and I'll hear all about it when I come in tomorrow. I expect I'll be asleep when it finishes tonight."

But it was difficult to sleep as strains of dance music drifted up to the dormitory. I'd never before really appreciated how Cinderella must have felt! I wondered what to do and eventually decided to go down to the Library to find some light reading to take my mind off the sadness that had crept over me. But I soon wished I hadn't as the corridor was full of handsome young men and unrecognisable sirens. I tried to pretend I was part of the drab wallpaper. I might as well have been as none of them paid the slightest attention to me. I didn't know whether to be relieved or sorry no one offered me the sympathy I felt I deserved.

Back in my room, clutching my Library book, I thought about the edict 'Thou shalt not dance.' It wasn't one of the ten commandments but the Brethren had introduced quite a few of their own. Of course they weren't the first to ban dancing on the grounds that it was 'worldly'. Hadn't Cromwell actually prohibited it by law? I wondered, resentfully, what was so 'wicked' about it.

"Well it's no good sitting here feeling sorry for yourself," I said firmly.

I got ready for bed and put on my dressing gown. Then, having made myself a reviving cup of cocoa in our small 'kitchen', I settled down to enjoy romance at second hand with Georgette Heyer's *Regency Buck*.

My friends were, of course, still asleep when I left the next morning for my second visit to Bognor. This time I felt I was going home. The weather was slightly cooler than the previous week but it was still sunny. I sat next to the same two sisters whose name was Lawrence. No one had invited me to lunch before I sat down so during the Meeting I'm afraid my mind wandered a little as I wondered whether I should have to return to College.

But as soon as the familiar clatter started, the lady sitting next to me, whispered, "Would you like to spend the day with us, dear?"

"Oh yes please," I responded with alacrity. "I should love to."

They were delightful ladies and reminded me of little birds as their tiny forms flitted along, heads nodding. Going into their small cottage was like stepping back into the nineteenth century. It was typical of many Brethren homes at that time. Dark Victorian furniture hid coyly under a clutter of china ornaments, the walls were covered with carefully worked samplers showing a variety of Biblical texts and the ladies themselves presided over lunch in the same courteous, gentle way as, I imagined, their mother and grandmother had done before them.

After lunch was over, the elder Miss Lawrence said gently, "We usually have a rest in the afternoon, dear. We thought we wouldn't go to the Reading today. I expect you're tired too, after all your hard work at College this week. Would you like to rest too? Or do you want to go to the Meeting? You can, of course, come back here for tea."

I hesitated. Would there be a black mark against me if I didn't go? My guilt complex, never far away, surfaced briefly but I pushed it firmly down. After all I hadn't slept very well the previous evening so I wasn't averse to a 'rest'.

"I think, perhaps, I would like to stay in this afternoon," I said hesitantly. "It has been rather a hectic week." Why did I have to make an excuse?

Miss Lawrence beamed. "I think that's a good idea. I'm sure the Lord expects us to rest sometimes. He won't expect us to rush around all the time, will he? Come along, dear. I'll show you to the guest room."

To my surprise, this contained a huge double bed.

"I hope you'll be comfortable," she said politely as if I was planning to stay for a week.

"Thank you. I'm sure I shall."

"There are some magazines by the bed." She gave me a warm smile and fluttered off.

I looked at the bedside table expecting to find some 'Brethren' literature and possibly some of Mr Darby's 'Ministry'. But to my delight a selection of women's magazines lay there, *Woman's Weekly, Good Housekeeping* and several others. I couldn't believe it! It was unheard of for sisters to read magazines and here I was being positively encouraged to do so. The Misses Lawrence obviously had hidden depths!

Slipping off my dress, I curled up under the voluminous eiderdown with the serial in *Woman's Weekly* but it didn't hold my attention and I was soon asleep. When I awoke, the house was very quiet. I sleepily unburied my arm to squint at my watch which said half past three. Picking up *Woman's Weekly*, which had slipped to the floor, I abandoned it in favour of *Good Housekeeping* and read until I decided it was time to make my reappearance.

Tea was delicious with home-made scones and fruit cake and then it was time for the Gospel Meeting. As there weren't brothers present, I was spared the ordeal of 'prayer for the Gospel'. That evening, to my delight, I was again invited to supper with the Earnshaws; after a lively singsong round the piano followed by some tasty 'nibbles', I sailed back to College accompanied by my two handsome escorts. This helped a little to alleviate my envy when I heard all about the 'fabulous' time Jean and Olive had had the previous evening!

There were other aspects of College life also forbidden to me. The College was under the auspices of the Church of England; Chapel Services were held regularly but they weren't compulsory so I didn't attend them. But I was intrigued by what went on and occasionally wondered whether I dared creep in at the back 'just to watch'. Was the Church of England really as black as she was painted by the Brethren? To attend a Church or Chapel service was un-heard of and I was surprised there hadn't been reaction to my training at a Church of England College. Perhaps the hierarchy hadn't realised! But I knew they'd thoroughly disapprove if they knew I'd been to a Chapel service.

However, unlike some stricter Brethren, I had at least been inside a Church although never, of course, to a service. My father had taken me to St. Paul's Cathedral and West-minster Abbey and sometimes, on holiday, we'd visited old village Churches. My father justified these excursions on the grounds they were 'educational' and I certainly wasn't going to argue with him.

Away from my home base and in a city where there was no Meeting, I wondered if I might be able to attend at least one Church service and I was pleased when an opportunity arose. A Dedication Service was to be held in Chichester Cathedral and, although not compulsory, it was expected all students would attend. I did some desultory conscience searching and then phoned home.

"There's a Dedication Service at Chichester Cathedral next week," I told my mother. "I'd like to go. Do you think I could? It's not compulsory but I think they expect us to be there."

"Well … I don't know … " I could almost hear my mother's brain ticking.

"Please."

"You'll have to ask Daddy." She adroitly passed the buck—and the phone—to my father.

I explained the situation again. There was a pause. "I don't see why not," he said at last. "You won't be taking Communion or anything, will you?"

I was taken aback. "But I couldn't, could I? Don't you have to be—confirmed or something?"

"Yes, yes, of course you do. I forgot. Well I hope you enjoy it—and don't forget to tell us all about it."

"The Bishop of Chichester's going to preach. I've never seen a Bishop before. Will he be dressed up, do you think?"

He laughed. "You'll have to wait and see."

He was! We arrived early at the Cathedral and I sat between Jean and Olive. The majestic building, which had seen so many centuries of worship, filled me with awe and I was impressed by the stately procession that glided up the aisle as the organ swelled out. The Bishop wore his mitre and an intricately embroidered cope. I was intrigued he carried a shepherd's crook and remembered Jesus, the Good Shepherd, had told the Apostle Peter to 'feed (his) lambs'. Tears hovered as I realised for the first time how the history of two thousand years of Christianity was still kept alive in the traditions of the Anglican Church. I hastily reminded myself Mr Darby had said the clerical system was wrong but at that moving moment, I wasn't convinced.

The Bishop's sermon was inspiring. He reminded us that, as teachers, we had a great responsibility as we held the future of the country in our hands. As Christians, we must keep the lamp of the Gospel burning and maintain high moral standards to set an example to our pupils. I left the Cathedral feeling perhaps I had chosen the right profession after all!

A few weeks later, I saw the Bishop again. This time it was in the College Chapel at a Confirmation Service. Jean was one of the candidates being confirmed.

"You will come, won't you?" she'd asked Olive and me one evening when we were lounging on my bed drinking cocoa.

"Yes, of course." Olive's reply was prompt.

I hesitated. "I should like to, Jean, but ... well, you know ... "

She understood. I was grateful for the undemanding friendship shown me at College. Never was I made to feel 'peculiar' or 'odd' if I refused to do things the other girls did. Soon after I'd met them, I'd explained the situation to Olive and Jean and they'd accepted it.

"If you can come, I'd be very pleased but if you decide not to, I'll quite understand," Jean told me.

I phoned my parents again and to my astonishment, they agreed I could go.

"But don't tell anyone, will you?" worried my mother. She meant, of course, anyone 'in the Meeting'.

"Of course not!" I exclaimed, horrified.

"And remember you mustn't take Communion," my father reminded me.

I was glad I went. It was an inspiring service and I was moved by the beautiful words in the Book of Common Prayer. Although I could understand why the Brethren felt an informal service and extempore prayers were more in keeping with the pattern of the early church, on that bright November day I was impressed by the ordered ritual of the service and the quiet reverence of the congregation.

Jean, like the other candidates, wore a simple white dress which flared out round her ankles and her head was covered by a veil. She looked lovely and I felt a lump in my throat as I watched the Bishop place his hands lightly on her head.

Communion followed and Olive, who'd already been confirmed, tiptoed past me to join the line that was moving to the altar. I sat and watched, feeling sad I couldn't take part in this celebration of the Lord's Supper. Surely, I thought, anyone who loved the Lord Jesus should be able to partake of his Supper with any group of Christians. Why were there so many man-made restrictions? The Breaking of Bread in the Meeting on Sunday mornings was often uplifting but somehow it lacked the feeling of awe and reverence that was almost tangible in this College Chapel. It was a time of worship I would not forget.

The term was drawing to a close and I was looking forward to the Christmas dinner that was to be held on the last night of term. This was one social occasion from which I wasn't barred and at last I should be able to fulfil one of my ambitions and wear a long evening dress. I'd saved some of my grant to buy one. I wanted something I would be able to remember for it might, after all, be the only time I should ever wear one.

At last I found one I liked and modelled it for Jean and Olive. Below a strapless top, yellow net billowed out over a taffeta underskirt. Gold sandals and a pearl necklace completed my ensemble. My only other jewellery was a gold signet ring my parents had given me for my eighteenth birthday.

I twirled round in front of my friends and dropped them a curtsey.I felt good and thoroughly enjoyed their compliments.

"You look gorgeous," said Olive. "What a pity you can't wear a little make up. Don't you think you could for once? You can borrow some of mine."

I hesitated and then decidedly shook my head. That was a step I didn't feel I could take. The Brethren still had a nineteenth century view of 'painted women' and I knew even my liberal parents would have been horrified.

The day of the dinner was crisp and cold but I was too excited to worry about the cold as I dressed in my finery. The College was centrally heated and it was the first winter I hadn't had chilblains. I twisted my long hair into a French pleat instead of my usual bun and then went to survey myself in the long mirror in the communal bathroom. I approved of what I saw and felt like Bishop Otter's answer to Elizabeth

Taylor! Shutting my eyes, I tried to imagine I was going to a Ball where I would meet my Prince Charming.

"Are you ready?" Olive in a lime green sheath shimmered in and we admired each other before sweeping down the stairs to the dining room which glittered with festive decorations and glamorously dressed females. The resident Chaplain, sole male lecturer and our one male student looked very drab in the midst of this bevy of beauty.

The Christmas dinner was superb and we were even given a glass of wine—an unheard of luxury. At least that was one thing about which I need feel no guilt. Surprisingly few of the Brethren were teetotallers. Hadn't St. Paul, himself, instructed Timothy to 'take a little wine for (his) stomach's sake'?

After coffee had been served, some of the girls lit cigarettes. I was relieved neither Jean nor Olive smoked. I was quite happy with the Brethren ban on that particular habit. Fortunately no one at our table lit up so we were spared the tobacco fumes that were swirling round other tables.

The unaccustomed wine had made us all slightly merry so, for once, leaving the debris of the meal on the table, we joined up to do a 'hokey-kokey'. We circled the dining room and then danced down the corridor and into the courtyard where we wove in and out among the cars. Some of the lecturers were trying to drive home but they good-humouredly put up with our high spirits.

It was late when we got to bed and I had to be up early to catch the train home for the Christmas holidays. All the way home—in the guard's van because the train was so crowded—I relived the previous evening and the feel of my glamorous evening dress billowing out round my ankles. I did hope I should be able to wear it again. I loved dressing up.

Chapter Seven

You Can Put The Ring On Now

T he Spring term hurtled by like something demented. I enjoyed the work but it was very demanding. We knew that in the 1960s the course would be increased to three years so we resented having to do three years' work in two. I found the Physical Education particularly exhausting although Modern Educational Dance was a new experience.

But English was stimulating and my love of Shakespeare increased. Miss Hill was a dynamic lecturer who read us the entire script of *Hamlet*. She obviously couldn't bear the thought of her students murdering the Bard's poetry. It was my first acquaintance with one of his most famous plays and it has remained my favourite.

Towards the end of the term, she announced she'd decided the first year English group would put on a small show for Open Day in June.

"I've given it a great deal of thought," she told us, "and I've decided we'll do a presentation of Milton's Masque *Comus*. The cloisters will be an ideal setting and we'll use some of the P.E. group to do the dances. The Art Department will make the masks and the Music Department will be responsible for the music so four departments will be involved."

Her enthusiasm was infectious and I wondered if I'd be involved. Dare I take part? I knew what the Brethren would say, but they didn't have to know, I thought smugly. Who was going to tell them? Certainly not Miss Smith, the Exclusive sister, who'd made it quite clear she wasn't in the least interested in my activities.

"Are you listening, Marion?" Miss Hill's voice broke into my thoughts and I blushed. She was the only one of our lecturers who called us by our first names.

"I'm sorry, Miss Hill," I muttered.

"I'll repeat what I've just said for your benefit." Her eyes glittered into mine and I felt hot enough to melt into the floor. I wished I could. It was a great trial to be so sensitive but if I was ever rebuked, I worried about it for days. I gazed fixedly at Miss Hill in order to redeem myself.

"You'll all audition for the main parts," she continued. "Milton's a very fine poet and it's important to widen your horizons. By the time we do the show in June, you'll know the Masque very well."

I didn't even know what a masque was but I was too embarrassed to ask. I assumed everyone else knew and only I was ignorant.

"You may take these copies. Please read it before tomorrow's lecture. I suggest you practise reading it aloud. I'll start to audition tomorrow. Good morning ladies," and she swept out leaving us slightly bewildered.

"What's a masque, anyway?" asked Olive.

"I wondered that, too," I admitted. "We'd better look it up."

The dictionary definition was, 'Amateur dramatic and musical entertainment especially in the sixteenth and seventeenth centuries, originally in dumb show, later with metrical dialogue.'

"I suppose that means a sort of poetry play with music," mused Jean.

"And dancing. Don't forget that." Doreen, who, like me, was a P.E. specialist did a pirouette around the room.

"Come on, Marion," said Olive. "Let's go and have coffee. We're free till lunch aren't we? We can read it together."

We didn't understand much of it but managed to untangle the storyline from the very flowery verse. The Lady, the main character, was lured into his lair by Comus who was determined to tarnish her purity. She underwent great tribulation and mocking by his hideous slaves before being finally released from his evil spell.

By now, I was as enthusiastic as Miss Hill and my overriding ambition in life was to play the Lady. If I could do that, I told myself, I would be resigned to the fact that never again would I be able to 'tread the boards'. The Brethren would certainly not look kindly upon a sister becoming an actress!

Olive listened patiently as I read the lines remembering all my elocution lessons at school.

"I think you need a bit more expression," she said critically when I paused for breath. "You read it very well but somehow there's no feeling. She's supposed to be frightened, isn't she?"

My friend wasn't supposed to be criticising me! She was there as an admiring audience. I opened my mouth to defend my rendering of Milton's poetry but shut it again. Of course she was right. I'd learned my first lesson. To act or write well I had to accept criticism if I was to improve. At home my recitations for friends, usually liberal brethren, had always met with uncritical applause.

"Thanks, Olive," I said at last. "You're right, of course. Can I try again?"

"That's much better," she approved when I'd finished. I felt as if I'd been given a diamond necklace. I blushed—with pleasure this time.

I could hardly wait for the auditions the next day. Impatiently, I listened to the efforts of the others and at last it was my turn. Moving in a dream to the front of the class, I took a deep breath. Then, as I read, the classroom faded away. I *was* the Lady taunted by Comus's 'ugly headed monsters'. I was no longer merely reading. I felt the lines. They came from inside me.

My legs were shaking as I moved back to my place and forced myself to return to the twentieth century. I didn't hear anyone else read. I was still wrapped in the Lady's identity.

"Thank you all very much, ladies," said Miss Hill eventually. "You've obviously all worked very hard. I'll let you know my decision tomorrow."

I'd never known time go so slowly. To concentrate on anything else was impossible. By now, any thoughts of the 'evils' of 'play acting' had been completely submerged and all I could think of was how much I wanted to play the Lady.

The next day I sat beside Olive, my heart pounding, as I waited to hear my fate.

Miss Hill didn't keep us waiting long. "You all read extremely well," she said. "I'm sorry some of you will be disappointed but you'll all take part as chorus, singers and dancers. Now the main part, the Lady. I've decided Marion should play it. She read it beautifully and really felt it."

She beamed at me and I almost burst with pride. I wanted to leap around the classroom screaming in ecstasy. But I managed to restrain myself and gave her a big smile as I said with deep feeling, "Oh thank you, Miss Hill."

Doreen was to play Comus, and Kay, who had a beautiful singing voice, would play the Spirit and eventually release me from evil.

"You don't mind not having a main part do you?" I asked Olive as we were drinking cocoa that evening.

She laughed. "Of course not, silly. I'm not nearly so enthusiastic as you are. I'm quite happy to be one of the crowd."

"It may be my only chance to do anything like this," I said sadly. "You know the Brethren's views on acting."

"Have you told your parents yet?"

"I phoned them this evening—slightly apprehensively. But they were thrilled for me."

"Will they be able to come?"

"Oh yes. They wouldn't miss it for anything. Oh, Olive, I'm so excited. I'm glad I've got the holidays to learn my lines."

I spent most of the Easter vacation glued to the text, rehearsing different ways of saying the lines. Then it was the summer term—always my favourite. But I had a problem. The College played both cricket and tennis and I was delighted to be picked for both teams. Then came the blow! Carol, the cricket captain, came to see me. She was obviously embarrassed.

"You bat really well, Marion," she said.

I beamed, proudly, and waited for her to continue. But there was an awkward pause and I was puzzled.

"Is there something wrong, Carol?" I asked as she didn't say anything.

"Well—er—yes, sort of." She cleared her throat. "You see students don't usually try for both teams and—er—well I'm afraid it's one of the College rules that you can't play in both. You have to choose."

"Oh, I see. I didn't know that." I was very disappointed.

"I realise you didn't but I'm afraid you have to decide. Julie asked me to see you." Julie was the tennis captain.

"You're certainly good enough for both tennis and cricket teams but the decision has to be yours."

"Do I have to decide right now?"

"Oh no. Early next week will do. There aren't any matches yet."

"Thanks."

All thoughts of *Comus* were driven out of my head as I pondered this momentous decision. I loved both sports and would have liked to continue with cricket as I'd been told I could have had a future in the England cricket team. But, of course, the Brethren wouldn't allow that and I'd made my decision to abide by their rules when I'd asked to Break Bread.

I sighed as I sat on my bed, thinking. There were far more prospective tennis players than there were cricket, I reflected, so there was more competition to get into the tennis team. Eventually, after much heart searching, I decided that 'College Tennis Team' would carry more weight on an application form than 'College Cricket Team'. So sadly my cricketing career came to an end. But my tennis continued to flourish and the following year I became tennis captain and even won the College singles tournament. After I left College, I couldn't join any clubs but I continued to play whenever I could at the schools where I taught so my tennis didn't get too rusty.

The next few weeks were the busiest I'd ever known. We played matches every Saturday, rehearsed *Comus* every free moment and in June we had a month of Teaching Practice. This was like doing two days' work in one. We taught and observed during the day and then at night we had to prepare detailed lessons for the next day. By the time it was over, I was completely exhausted.

I conscientiously continued to attend the Meeting at Bognor on Sundays. The Brethren were very good to me and were not even critical when I often decided to rest instead of attending the Reading. It was the only time I was able to relax and I needed the sleep I was able to snatch on Sunday afternoons.

Comus was beginning to take shape and we started to rehearse outside in the cloisters. It was a beautiful setting with the stately grey stone behind us and the green lawn sweeping down to the colourful garden in front of us. The masks that the Art department had made were very effective. The first time they were worn, I disgraced myself.

"Who are these—these ugly-headed monsters?" I quavered, turning my head just as one of the 'monsters' thrust its ugly visage close to my face. I dissolved into laughter. Once I'd started, I couldn't stop and soon Lady and monsters were rolling around in paroxysms of mirth. Miss Hill had great difficulty in restoring order.

At last came the day of the dress rehearsal and with it the moment of truth. We had to wear make up! All the gremlins of my upbringing surged round me making as ugly faces as the 'monsters' who tormented me in the Masque.

"I don't want to wear make up," I wailed. "I've never worn it."

"Of course you have to wear it," said Miss Hill, briskly. "It's to accent your features. The audience will be some distance away and they won't be able to see you properly without it."

My conscience fought a losing battle. I hadn't really any choice, I told myself. And no one would know!

"All right," I sighed. "But I don't know anything about it. Can someone put it on for me?"

"Yes, of course. June, you're one of the best with make up. Come and do the leading lady."

I swelled with pride. Me—a leading lady. My goodness! What would Mr Wickens have said? I sobered. Needles of guilt pricked me. Why was it I always had to feel so guilty about anything I did?

Under June's ministrations I almost went to sleep. It was very soothing having my face stroked and patted. All I had to do was relax. I enjoyed it.

"Lean forward." I obeyed and June fluffed some powder on to my face. "You look quite different. Go and look in the mirror."

For a moment I couldn't believe it was me. Was I really this glamorous beauty staring solemnly back at me? What a difference make up made. My hair was piled on top of my head instead of being scraped back in my usual bun and when I donned the cream toga bordered with gold and fastened with a large gold brooch, I looked every inch the Roman lady.

The rehearsal went well. Afterwards I was quite sorry to have to remove the make up. I approved of the improvement it had made to my appearance. I was impatient for the next day and the performances. There was to be one in the afternoon and one in the evening.

My parents came in the morning and I met them at the station. We had an early lunch and as I was leaving to prepare for my big moment, I said casually, "Oh, by the way, I have to wear make up. I thought I'd better warn you."

I ran off before they could make any response. The dressing room was buzzing and June was waiting impatiently, grease paint poised. Her efforts were even more spectacular this time and as I waited for my entrance, I knew I looked good and was well prepared. But that didn't help the butterflies that were doing a tap dance in my stomach. In a dream I floated out to the cloisters, vaguely aware of crowds of people all looking at me. I tried to say my opening lines but my voice seemed to have disappeared and my memory had forsaken me. I took a deep breath as I said a quick prayer. It worked! The audience faded and then I was alone in a dark cavern with my tormentor.

Comus is definitely an acquired taste but the audience's reception of our offering was gratifying and I allowed myself a relieved smile as I took my bow and managed to catch my parents' eyes.

"You were wonderful, darling," said my mother, as, returned to normality, I ran to receive their compliments.

"What a pity you won't be able to do any acting after you leave College," mused my father.

I didn't want to think about that. I wanted to savour to the full the present.

"Do you mind if I leave my make up on when we go out for tea?" I asked. "It takes so long to take it off and I need it on for this evening."

"Of course not," said my father. "You look very pretty, doesn't she, Rose?"

My mother agreed but I could sense a little reservation. She was probably worried in case we were seen by any Brethren.

The evening performance was even more successful and afterwards I think we were all sorry it was over and we wouldn't be giving any more performances. It seemed a great deal of work for only two of them. I'd thoroughly enjoyed my first taste of the theatre and was very sad that my acting career, like my cricketing one, was likely to be brief. Why was it that everything I liked to do was banned by the Brethren? The euphoria of my success in *Comus* was soon replaced by resentment that I couldn't use this particular talent that God, himself, surely had given me. But I kept quiet. I didn't want to upset my parents and, after all, the Brethren were always right, weren't they?

With the end of term came the Physical Education camping trip in the New Forest. This was a new experience and not one that appealed to me much. I liked my comforts! The inside of our tent resembled a jungle but after we'd hacked at the worst of it, there was some improvement and I slept very well in spite of the uneven ground. Fortunately, apart from a thunderstorm on the first evening, we had gorgeous weather. The second night was so hot some of us slept outside. I liked the feeling of nothing between me and the stars. But I didn't like the insects. Every species had apparently made a special trip to visit our camp. There were hornets, wasps, flies, ants and one morning we were jerked awake by a shriek from Doreen who'd found a lizard crawling over her!

However the week wasn't as bad as I'd anticipated, but I was still relieved to return to the comforts of home and an unlumpy bed.

A few weeks after we returned for our second year, it was my twenty first birthday. I wanted to make it a special occasion and although I hadn't much money, I'd saved a little so Jean, Olive and Mair, a Welsh girl with whom I'd also become friendly, could go out for dinner.

I'd bought a turquoise taffeta dress with a sweet heart neckline and felt very glamorous as I clasped around my neck the sparkling necklace my friends had given me. It was a crisp November night as we walked down to the town to the Ship Hotel where I'd booked a table. I felt rather apprehensive as it was my first experience of the 'high life'. So far my eating out had been restricted to 'tea' at Lyons Corner House.

However, I was determined to behave as if I did this all the time so we swept into the bar as I'd decided it was correct to have a drink first—even if it was only pineapple juice! The table was booked for eight o'clock so just before that time, I led my friends into the restaurant.

"I've booked a table for four," I announced grandly.

"Name please."

"Miss Field."

"This way please, Madam."

We followed our guide though the candlelit dining room to a corner table. He pulled out a chair for me and I nearly had an accident as I sat down before he was ready. However, some adroit juggling on his part landed me on the seat and I smiled graciously as he shook out the napkin and placed it on my lap. This was the life, I thought. I could get used to this. He handed us a menu which we studied studiously. It was very expensive. I hoped I'd have enough money.

"Would you like some wine with your meal, Madam?" The wine waiter hovered near us.

"Yes please." I took the wine list and stared at it. So far my sole acquaintance with that beverage was in the privacy of my own home and I couldn't tell one wine from another. But I certainly wasn't going to admit it. I tried to look intelligent and then had an inspiration.

"Could you recommend something please." Then, greatly daring, I added, "Not too expensive please."

"Of course, Madam. What are you going to eat?"

I couldn't think what that had to do with it but didn't wish to appear ignorant.

"Well—er—I'm not sure. Er—have you chosen yet?"

"I'll have the chicken," announced Olive promptly.

"So will I," chorused Jean and Mair. Chicken was my favourite meat so I had no difficulty in making up my mind.

The waiter beamed. "Then you'll want a white wine—with white meat," he added, obviously recognising our naivety. "I'd recommend this one. It's very popular."

"Right, we'll have a bottle of that, then." I sighed with relief as I passed the first hurdle. Ordering the chicken presented no problem and we all had grapefruit to start.

When our first course had been cleared away, the wine waiter appeared again, reverently carrying the bottle of white wine which he presented to me. Smiling graciously, I attempted to take it from him. I was startled when this resulted in a tug of war which fortunately he won before our antics resulted in the bottle being smashed on the floor.

"Would you like to taste it, Madam?" he enquired, panting a little from his exertion. Then he obviously decided it would be better not to give me any other opportunity to display my ignorance and added diplomatically, "Or shall I just pour it for you?"

"Oh pour it, please," I gasped, still red in the face from my faux pas.

When our glasses had all been filled, Olive raised hers. "Let's drink a toast," she said. "To Marion. Happy birthday and may you have many more."

I beamed with pleasure. My social gaffe was forgotten and now I could relax and enjoy the meal. It was late when we returned to College, but the doors were open and we were still giggling with the effect of the unaccustomed wine.

The following Sunday I spent as usual in Bognor with Andrea and her family. As soon as we reached her home after the Meeting, she dragged me up to her bedroom.

"I've got something to show you," she cried. "Look!" She held out her left hand.

"Oh, Andrea, it's beautiful. Congratualtions. Who is he?" I gazed in awe at the solitaire diamond on her engagement finger.

"His name's Geoffrey. I met him last year on holiday. We're getting married in the summer. You must book the date now. It's June 5th. We're going to have a marquee in the garden. You must come with us to the Registry Office too. We're not inviting too many people to that but I'd like you to come."

"Thank you," I said, touched. "I should love to. It'll be a good excuse to buy a new dress too. What are you going to wear?"

She laughed. "It's a secret but I can tell you it will be white."

"Will it really?" I was surprised. The Brethren didn't go in for 'white weddings' and brides never wore veils. They dressed in ordinary dresses or suits with the usual hats. But they were often more glamorously attired than usual. Of course it was obligatory to marry someone 'in the Meeting'. I suddenly remembered hearing my six year old sister saying seriously to a playmate, "I can't marry you, Michael 'cos you don't go to the Meeting."

The Exclusive Brethren were also not licensed to hold weddings in their Meeting Rooms. They regarded the civil and the religious part of the marriage ceremony as separate so were always married in Registry Offices. Following this would be the reception—usually at the bride's home. In the afternoon there would be a 'Wedding Meeting' either in the local Meeting Room or in a hall—often surprisingly, a Church one. Those who hadn't been invited to the wedding would be able to attend the Meeting which would follow the pattern of a Fellowship Meeting with tea afterwards.

"Isn't it a pity you can't be married in the Meeting Room with a veil and everything?" I said wistfully as I lounged on Andrea's bed watching her do her hair which had escaped from its pins in her excitement.

"I don't really mind. It'll still be a day to remember."

"Oh, yes," I agreed but I wasn't convinced. I loved weddings and always stopped to watch if I passed a church when wedding photos were being taken. I was very envious of my mother who, in her teens, had actually been a bridesmaid at her step sister's wedding in a church! How she'd managed that when she was in the Brethren, I have no idea and neither has she.

For the rest of the day I'm afraid my mind was on the forthcoming wedding. It was the first time I'd been invited to one and I knew it would be as glamorous as the Brethren would allow. Andrea's parents were not poor and I was sure they'd give their only daughter an appropriate start to her new life.

The year continued to hurtle past and I became more and more tired. But I reserved some energy for choosing my ensemble for the wedding. I chose a pale green organdie dress speckled with dark green which flared over a full taffeta underskirt. It almost reached my ankles and I had a matching green hat with a wide brim. Long green nylon gloves almost reaching to the short puffed sleeves and matching shoes and handbag completed my outfit.

On the day of the wedding I felt rather conspicuous in my finery as I waited at the bus stop but I enjoyed the appreciative glances I received. The journey seemed to take longer than usual—presumbably because there was more traffic on a Saturday.

I reached Andrea's house in good time to find organised chaos. The marquee was being set up, caterers were rushing around, flowers were all over the place and Andrea was floating around in a pink satin negligee.

"You look lovely," she exclaimed kissing me. "Come and help me dress. Janice is upstairs. I think you met her once. She's my cousin and is going to be my bridesmaid."

She hurried me upstairs and I watched as Janice helped her into the white lace dress with a fitted bodice flaring out into an ankle length skirt. When she had added her wide brimmed white hat, she looked stunning. We followed her downstairs.

"You go in the car with the boys," her father instructed me. "We'll bring up the rear."

I found the Registry Office wedding a real anti climax. Andrea and her family in their glamorous clothes seemed to have no place in this drab building though I had to admit it would suit the dowdy clothes Brethren usually wore. But Andrea's family wasn't in the least dowdy and I felt sorry she couldn't have a more attractive setting for her wedding.

In the room into which we were ushered a bored bald-headed man looked up from behind a desk, peered at us over his glases, waved us to some seats and continued to write. He looked as though he had far better things to do than perform a marriage ceremony. Sandwiched between Andrea's brothers, I suddenly felt very uncomfortable. The silence seemed interminable and I wondered what we were waiting for.

At last Baldhead flung down his pen, reorganised his papers and stood up. "Which is the bride and groom?" he barked.

It seemed obvious to me but I supposed it would be a pity if he'd re-married Andrea's parents by mistake. Andrea and Geoffrey stood up and moved to stand in front of the desk. They were both tall so Baldhead almost disappeared behind them. He was obviously in a hurry and he raced through the words so fast I could hardly understand them. At last he stopped to draw breath and then announced, casually, "You can put the ring on now if you like."

I couldn't believe it. I'd always thought the ring was an important part of a wedding. Had this really been a binding marriage ceremony? It seemed so lacking in reverence. I found it hard to accept that the Brethren, who held such strict views on marriage and prohibited divorce, actually recognised this mockery of a 'ceremony'.

But no one else seemed to be reacting at all. I sighed. It must be me again. No doubt this was one more time when 'the Brethren knew best'. At least the marriage would be 'blest' at the afternoon Meeting, I reminded myself. I wondered wryly if the Brethren would recognise the marriage if something happened to prevent the Wedding Meeting.

Back at the house, the sun shone in the beautiful rose covered garden where we were handed glasses of champagne. I took a sip and decided it was vastly overrated. But the meal was delicious. I hadn't eaten so much for a long time. Although I was disappointed in the taste, I had two glasses of champagne. Unfortunately I'd drunk them both before I realised I needed some to drink a toast to the bride and groom. I wondered sadly if I'd ever learn to behave properly in polite society.

Hoping everyone was too busy looking at Andrea to notice me, I raised the glass to my lips and took a sip of air. I'd become quite proficient at this by the third toast but to my embarrassment I was found out and my glass was refilled. At least I had something to drink with my slice of wedding cake. By the time I staggered upstairs to make myself presentable for the Meeting, I was seeing everything through a rosy glow and had to be very careful where I put my feet.

I was given a lift to the Meeting by a couple I'd never met before. They were very friendly but I wasn't in a talkative mood. All I wanted to do was sleep. I hoped I wouldn't nod off in the Meeting and fall off my chair. If I'd been strong minded, I'd have refused the third glass of champagne, toast or not. But having been given it, my habit of thrift prohibited me from leaving a full glass.

The Meeting was held in the local Church Hall as there were so many guests, and the chairs were arranged in the usual square. All the Brethren from the Bognor Meeting were already there but seats had been reserved for the guests; by the time I sat down, the hall was full, apart from the front row which was reserved for the wedding party.

What a shame we didn't have an organ, I thought sadly as Andrea and her new husband made their way to the front seats followed by Janice and the rest of the relations. She should have walked in to the strains of the 'Wedding March'.

I had difficulty concentrating on the Meeting where the theme was naturally marriage—a state ordained by God. Andrea and Geoffry were prayed for, the passage describing the Wedding at Cana where Jesus turned water into wine, was read and discussed and various brothers read other passages from the Bible and commented on them.

Then it was time for tea which was far more elaborate than the usual 'Meeting tea'. Part of the wedding cake had also been brought to the hall so everyone was able to sample it. Like the reception, Andrea's father would have paid for the tea. It must have cost him a fortune, I reflected, munching my second slice of wedding cake. But at least he only had one daughter!

After the cake had been passed round, Andrea and Geoffrey disappeared to change. When they reappeared, Andrea was wearing a pale blue linen suit and matching straw hat. We waved them off on their new life together and suddenly life seemed very flat again.

"Come back and have some supper with us, dear," said Andrea's mother who was standing beside me.

"Oh may I? That would be lovely."

I didn't think I'd be able to eat any more but it would put off my return to the mundane life of College.

It took me a while to return to normality but final examinations were looming on the horizon so I had no time to daydream. Then suddenly it was all over. If my results were satisfactory, I would be a qualified teacher and ready to be unleashed on the unsuspecting children of the next generation.

Chapter Eight

A Real Theatre!

I passed my examinations achieving, to my delight, a credit in English and eventually obtained a post teaching Physical Education in a Secondary Modern school in Winchester. I'd rather have taught English but unfortunately there were too many English teachers chasing too few jobs. I'd also wanted to return home but my application to Surrey had been unsuccessful. I'd had an interview at County Hall but the authorities there had apparently not been very impressed with me.

It had been a frustrating interview. As always, when I had an appointment, I arrived well before the scheduled time. Half an hour after the interview time I was still waiting and when I was eventually called an hour later, the interviewer's first words were, "I suppose you were late!"

My indignant denial was obviously not believed and, thoroughly upset by this cavalier treatment, I certainly didn't appear to the best advantage. I discovered later that Surrey was never very interested in raw recruits just out of college so that fact soothed my wounded ego a little.

So, unsuccessful in my first choice of area, I was relieved when Winchester took the risk of offering me a post. Fortunately there was a Meeting in the city so I was able to accept it without any qualms. I knew I wouldn't have been allowed to work in a place where I couldn't attend the Meeting regularly.

I managed to rent a bed-sitting room for the sum of twelve pounds a month—almost half my pay. Having lived on a grant for two years, I enjoyed having a salary but twenty eight pounds a month still didn't allow me any luxuries. But I liked being independent and had soon scattered books, ornaments and photographs round my furnished room. My landlady was delightful and always ready for a chat. I needed someone to listen when I came home from my traumatic attempts to teach uninterested girls the intricacies of hockey and netball. I spent most of my time in the changing room persuading them to change into appropriate garments. The weather was getting cooler and they objected to replacing skirts and cardigans with the statutory short sleeved blouse and navy blue knickers.

"It's too cold, Miss," they'd wail, huddling against the radiator as I tried to shepherd them out into the frosty air.

Every day was a battle. I fared little better in the gymnasium where I found one small girl, Mary, a particular trial. She spent most of the lesson playing hide and seek amongst the apparatus. Sometimes she didn't even appear at the beginning of the lesson and I had to send out a search party for her. Occasionally she felt we could benefit from the accompaniment of a violin which was almost as big as she was. It was impossible to prise it from her grasp so I usually ended the lesson with a splitting headache after trying to shout above the very discordant 'tune' Mary insisted on playing.

My Saturday mornings were taken up with matches and I became more and more exhausted. Once again I wondered if I'd chosen the right profession. Certainly none of the girls I taught seemed the least interested in learning anything. I was very depressed and the thought of attempting to teach bored children for the next forty years was decidedly unattractive.

The only escape I thought gloomily one evening as I sat huddled over my electric fire, was if I had a husband to support me so I could give up work and stay at home. But there was no sign of such a gentleman on the horizon.

The Brethren at Winchester spoilt me in the same way as those at Bognor. There were fewer of them but they made me just as welcome and the Bests, a young couple with two small children became my adopted family. Andrew Best was tall, dark and handsome and I wondered sadly, why all the nicest brothers had to be already married before I met them!

Sundays were an oasis of peace in an otherwise exhausting life. The only thing that reconciled me to teaching was that I discovered I could hold the attention of the girls, even my *bête noire*, Mary, when I taught Dance. I hadn't enjoyed Modern Educational Dance at College but to my delight I discovered my pupils loved it.

I was amazed! I was helped and stimulated by a marvellous lady, Mrs Asher, who played the piano for me. Her magic fingers could produce sounds to stimulate any mood or situation I required.

"I want some battle music," I'd cry, as we recreated the battle of Troy. My love of Greek mythology had suddenly surfaced from my childhood as I realised the wealth of drama in the stories. Carried away by my success in this field, I even started a Dance Club for the most talented and on Open Day at the end of the year we produced a Dance Drama based on the story of Orpheus and Euridice. I was delighted when it was an overwhelming success and touched to be presented with my first bouquet.

Perhaps my dramatic talents weren't to be wasted after all, I thought smugly as I arranged them in my room that evening. I felt quite 'high' on the adulation I'd received from my colleagues and the parents. But the compliment I treasured most was from Miss Cartright, the County P.E. Inspector who'd sought me out to tell me how impressed she'd been that I'd produced something 'of such high quality' at the end of my first year of teaching. After the trauma of much of it, I was relieved I had, apparently, passed my probationary year and wouldn't be unemployed the following year.

Soon after I returned home for the Summer holidays, I received an unexpected visitor. This was the Headmaster of a local mixed Secondary Modern school.

"I have a Physical Education post going at my school, Miss Field," he stated without preamble. "I believe you are the right person to fill it."

I was delighted to be 'headhunted' so early in my career although I didn't think my first year of teaching had been an unqualified success. However, I wanted to live at home and I was certainly not very enamoured of my present school.

"That's very kind of you, Mr Granger," I said, "but I wouldn't be able to start till January would I? I have to give three months' notice."

"We're prepared to hold the post until then if you're interested. I do hope you are." His gimlet eyes glared into mine. It almost sounded like a threat.

I thought quickly. This was what I'd wanted but it would mean leaving my first post after only four terms. However, he'd searched me out. I didn't like to enquire how he'd found me but I presumed he'd received my details from the county authorities. They had plenty of data on me.

"Thank you very much, Mr Granger," I said after a short pause. "I'd like to accept your offer and I look forward to working in West Byfleet."

My current Headmistress was not impressed when I went to see her soon after the start of term. She eyed me disapprovingly.

"I suppose you want a testimonial," she remarked. "A year's not very long is it? Are you sure you want to go?"

"Yes I do, if you don't mind," I said politely.

"It won't look very good on applications forms, you know. Employers prefer applicants to stay longer in their first posts."

"I'm sorry," I said. She was obviously not going to make it easy for me.

"Very well. I'll have your testimonial ready for you by the end of the week but I can't say very much about you."

"Thank you, Miss Hickson." I escaped, feeling about an inch high. She was right, of course, but it still seemed right to move as Mr Granger had actually offered me a post in the county which had originally been my first choice. The reference, when I received it, said very little except that I 'might make a good teacher one day'.

The following week my thoughts were given a new direction when I was called to the office to take a phone call. This was so unusual I immediately thought the worst. Had there been an accident? Was one of my parents ill?

I hurtled in and the secretary looked startled. "Don't look so worried, dear," she said. "It's Miss Cartright."

Help! Had I failed my year after all? Or had I done something else wrong? Had Mrs Jones at last complained. as she was always threatening to do, that I'd forced her darling daughter into the icy cold wearing hardly any clothes?

I took several deep breaths and picked up the phone. "Good morning, Miss Cartright," I said politely.

"Good morning, Miss Field. I'm sorry to drag you away from your class but I won't keep you long. I've just had a call from the Southern Region Opera Company. They're doing a production of Gounod's *Faust* at the end of November. They're well into rehearsal but the director's decided he'd like some children to play the angels who surround Marguerite as she goes to Heaven. There'll be a little dance involved so I immediately thought of you. Do you think you could train some of your little dancers for this?"

I was speechless. I couldn't believe it. I, an Exclusive sister, was being asked to be involved in a real live theatre production!

"Miss Field? Are you still there?"

"Oh yes," I gasped. "I, I—oh … er—thank you Miss Cartright."

"So you'll do it?"

She wasn't giving me any time to decide. Thoughts clouded my mind. Would the Brethren find out? Dare I do it?

"I'd love to," I heard myself say. Of course I'd never really had any intention of turning down this marvellous opportunity. At that moment I was even prepared to be 'withdrawn from' if my 'sin' was discovered.

For the rest of the day I was in a daze. In the evening I phoned my parents and, rather apprehensively, told them the news.

"Oh dear," said my mother.

"But it's a marvellous opportunity," I pleaded, adding cunningly, "No one'll find out."

My father was more enthusiastic. After all I was over twenty one and I was now responsible for my own decisions. But it was still very hard to dent, even slightly, the mould that constricted my life. I knew I wanted the challenge of training my dancers for the Opera but I knew also I would suffer the inevitable feelings of guilt as I did so. But I couldn't turn down a chance like this.

The children were as delighted as I was and when we were actually rehearsing, I was totally involved and any guilt feelings were submerged. When I walked to the theatre for the final rehearsals, it was dark and I couldn't help looking behind me to make sure no stray brothers were dogging my footsteps, ready to report me for taking part in such a 'worldly' activity.

I met the children at the theatre and once I'd checked they were all present, we made our way to the auditorium. The stage was ablaze with lights and festooned with ladders, tools and other unidentifiable objects. The leading lady, ignoring the chaos all around her, was singing. Taking a deep breath, I moved forward followed by the children. The soprano came to the end of her aria, shaded her eyes against the brilliant lights and peered down at us.

"Are those my angels that I see there?" she cried enthusiastically. "Welcome darlings. We've been waiting for you."

Oh dear! Surely we weren't late. A man loomed up in front of me.

"Miss Field. I'm Gerry Noakes, the Director. It's awfully good of you to come."

"We were thrilled to be asked. I do hope we're not late."

"Oh no. We're not quite ready yet. We've got to get the steps fixed. Can they work on those?"

He waved his hand at the stage and I realised the 'ladder' I'd noticed was actually steps leading up to 'Heaven'. We'd practised on something similar so it shouldn't be difficult, I assured him.

For the next couple of hours we worked hard, perfecting the movements on the stage and adjusting to the soloist who was a great encouragement and very appreciative of the work we'd done. I thoroughly enjoyed myself. But although I was concentrating hard, I still had a thought to spare for my daring in actually being involved in a real theatre. I hoped very much no Brethren would get to hear of my escapade. I dreaded to think of the consequences if they did.

My guilt complex was still trying to push its way to the surface but so far I'd succeeding in smothering it with my excitement.

However, it did make a meteoritic leap when I discovered we were required for the dress rehearsal on the following Sunday afternoon. On the Sunday morning I found it hard to concentrate as I was trying to perfect the excuse to offer when the Bests invited me to lunch.

"It's very kind of you," I gushed when Jenny made her usual offer, "but would you mind if I didn't come today? I, … I'm rather tired and I'm afraid I do have quite a lot of school work to do." That was half true, I thought.

She gave me an odd look but then smiled and patted my shoulder.

"That's quite all right, dear," she said kindly. "I quite understand. Another time perhaps."

"Thank you." I clattered down the stairs from the small Meeting Room which had once been a Victorian school. I wanted to get away before too many questions were asked.

When we arrived at the theatre, the stage had been transformed into Faust's study. We watched, enthralled, as the opera progressed. All the soloists had beautiful voices and I was impressed with the movements of the chorus.

"I'd love to do choreography for an opera," I thought wistfully. But of course the door to the backstage area was as firmly closed as that to the stage.

I sighed and tried to concentrate on Faust's dilemma. My guilt feelings were more in evidence today because it was Sunday and the idea of Faust selling his soul to the devil was one, I felt, that perhaps justified the Brethren's view of the 'worldly' theatre. Perhaps I shouldn't have been involved. Suppose someone saw me coming out of the theatre after the rehearsal. By now, I'd worked myself into such a state that I missed our entrance and the rehearsal was held up while I shepherded the girls backstage. Embarrassment was now added to the guilt in my emotional cauldron and my face was as red as the lights flashing around the unhappy doctor. I couldn't wait to get home. Why had I ever become involved? Fortunately the 'angel' scene progressed without any more hitches and I hoped everyone would forget our late arrival on stage.

We had a 'rest' from rehearsing on the Monday so I assuaged my conscience by going to the Prayer Meeting although I was very tired and would much rather have stayed at home. For the rest of the week I kept my guilt firmly buttoned down. I was delighted to be allowed to stay backstage during the performances and greedily absorbed the emotive atmosphere. How I wished I was out under the lights—even as a member of the chorus.

The week ended far too quickly for me. Life felt so flat and uninteresting with no dance rehearsals and no performances. I could only daydream now. The likelihood of my ever being involved in any productions again seemed very remote.

The rest of the term went by very quickly. Then it was the Christmas holidays and my chapter in Winchester was over. During this time I'd been vaguely aware that things weren't quite right in the Brethren but with my propensity for burying my head in the sand, I hadn't tried to identify the problem. Besides, I'd been too busy directing dancers, trying unsuccessfully to convince my pupils it wasn't cold, adding up registers, dealing with first aid and doing the hundred and one other things required of a teacher.

So I'd only heard very faint rumblings of the brewing storm that was waiting to turn my life and many others upside down within the next few years.

Chapter Nine

Break Up!

The mixed Secondary Modern where I went to teach Physical Education in the New Year was a great improvement on the one I'd left. It was firmly under the control of the Headmaster who told me he ran 'a very tight ship'. He certainly did. The pupils were terrified of him and so were some of the staff—including me!

But his tight reins meant that at least I didn't have to shout myself hoarse before I could achieve some semblance of peace in the gymnasium. In my first lesson I was so startled by the complete silence that followed my 'stop', my brain went into shock and I couldn't think what to say next!

Unfortunately, however, the girls' changing room was not far from the Head's office and he was allergic to noise. One day he erupted into the cloakroom, where the class was changing, to announce angrily he couldn't hear himself think. The girls' chattering seemed to me considerably quieter than that coming from the boys at the other end of the corridor but, of course he couldn't hear that from his room. My teenage pupils, quite justifiably, objected to this male visitation and, after he'd stormed out, demanded I complain. Having 'screwed my courage to the sticking place', I did so but was told our lord and master was 'in a privileged position and therefore different from other men'! Later I thought of several appropriate replies to that!

I found my work still tiring but I had a little energy left over to take stock of my future. Clubs, sports, the theatre and other delights were still banned to me but I was determined to make the most of what wasn't taboo. Now I was living at home, I could save a little more money and I decided to take driving lessons. We still had no car but one of the young brothers from the Meeting kindly allowed me to practise in his. It was very brave of him as he must have nearly suffered a heart attack on many occasions!

But my favourite hobby was writing. I'd written stories ever since I could remember and I wondered if I might avoid the Brethren taboo by using a pen name if I was ever published. Surreptitiously I read any women's magazines I could find. I was sure I could write stories as good as those that were published!

I'd recently written a love story called 'Silver Lining' and, greatly daring, I submitted it to *Woman's Own*. Then I waited for weeks until it finally came homing back to me like a wounded pigeon.

Nothing daunted, I enrolled in a correspondence Writers' course. This was a considerable help as I learned a great deal about the mechanics of writing. I'd had no idea how to submit a manuscript. I hadn't even used double spacing! I enjoyed the course but sadly it didn't result in any sales. Perhaps love stories weren't really my forte. After all what did I know of romantic love—or life either—wrapped in my cosy cocoon?

Meanwhile my father, who like me, suffered from shyness, had enrolled in a Dale Carnegie course on 'How to win friends and influence people'. Naturally the Brethren wouldn't have approved but fortunately it was held on Tuesday evenings when there wasn't a Meeting. He thoroughly enjoyed it and definitely acquired more self confidence so when another course was started, I joined it.

We had to give talks to the rest of the group; sometimes these were prepared and sometimes impromptu. On the last day of the course there was a competition and the best speaker of the evening would win a Dale Carnegie pencil. I couldn't believe it when my name was called out as the winner and I was presented with the beautiful grey pencil with the words 'Highest award for achievement' engraved on it. My father was delighted and it certainly gave a boost to my self confidence.

So did passing my driving test at the second attempt. Having done this, I bought myself a very old, very large and very inexpensive car. I was extremely proud of it although it was far too heavy for me and the first time I took it out alone, I wrapped it round a lamppost and had to be extricated by a passer-by! Fortunately, my ego was more dented than the car.

Soon after this we moved house. We didn't go far. We transferred to a larger house 'just round the corner'. We had a van to move the furniture but we carried up our clothes and small items. The house had been empty for some time so we could take our time to move in. My maternal grand-mother, recently widowed, moved in with us and had a room on the ground floor. She had her meals with us and although she was in her eighties and her bulk prevented her moving easily, she was in full possession of all her faculties.

My sister was following in my footsteps at a Teachers' Training College in Bristol where, as elsewhere, the course had now been extended to three years. The Bristol Brethren were as welcoming to her as the Bognor Brethren had been to me. She'd been Breaking Bread for two years and she told us she was excited about attending some three day Meetings in the city.

We were happy for her but my father was becoming increasingly uneasy about some of the things happening among the Brethren. Like him, I'd expected to remain within the Exclusive Brethren all my life. I was aware there were other Christians 'in the world' but the persistent needling that only our group had 'the Light' while the rest were 'in darkness' had probed so deeply into my subconscious it was difficult to dislodge.

I was also very naïve about 'the facts of life' and in many ways saw the Brethren through rose coloured spectacles. I might sometimes resent some of the rules that hampered my life style but on the whole I respected them and in spite of their odd ideas, it never occurred to me to doubt their morals. Even the 'world' recognised the upright nature of these 'unworldly' citizens.

It came as a great shock to me, therefore, to discover some of them had feet of clay. Soon after the start of term, I planned to spend a weekend in Winchester but, to my surprise, I was advised by the Woking Brethren not to go. No reason was given so naturally I assumed I'd 'sinned' again in some way. Or was there, perhaps, a new rule that sisters weren't allowed to go away for weekends?

"I don't understand it," I said to my father. "What have I done wrong now?"

He looked embarrassed. "I don't think it's anything to do with you, darling."

He didn't elaborate but I refused to be put off.

"What is it to do with then?" I demanded truculently.

"I'm afraid there's some trouble in Winchester at the moment."

"Trouble? What sort of trouble?"

My father cleared his throat. He was obviously not finding the conversation easy. I waited. At last he gave an answer that shattered my protective glass case beyond repair.

"I'm afraid Julian West has been having an affair with Susan Ricks."

"Having an affair?" The terminology was so unlike anything I'd ever heard from my father, it took a while for me to understand it. When I did, I felt as though I'd been given a vicious blow in the stomach. "I don't believe it."

"I'm afraid it's true. It must have started while you were there."

I collapsed into an arm chair trying to create some sort of order out of the shattered images exploding in my mind. I felt sick. I knew both Julian West and Susan Ricks. Julian had only been married a year. But Brethren didn't have 'affairs'. That was something the 'world' did. Not the Brethren. The Brethren were always right—weren't they? Suddenly doubts that had become blurred over the years were in sharp focus. I gasped as if I'd been plunged into an ice cold swimming pool.

"I'm sorry, darling. I knew it would be a shock for you." My father's voice came from a distance.

Then abruptly I resurfaced and started to laugh hysterically. This was the stuff of black comedy.

"Oh dear," I gasped. "Fancy a brother ... they've always been so—so—pompous—and—and—self righteous."

"Pull yourself together, Marion," said my father sharply. "It's not the end of the world."

But it was the beginning of the end of our world. This event was being duplicated elsewhere in our very 'upright' sect and coupled with later misinterpretations of the Bible, the Exclusive Brethren finally crashed off their self-erected pedestal.

However, this was not the only shock of its kind I was to receive. An unexpected staff meeting was called one evening after school and to my horror, the Headmaster announced two members of staff had been 'having an affair' and had both been dismissed. I'd recently become friendly with Barbara, a young Roman Catholic teacher on the staff.

We were both equally naïve and I cried all the way home. But worse was to come. The next morning we arrived at school to learn the male half of the affair had committed suicide in his classroom. It seemed like a nightmare as Barbara and I walked out of school trying to dodge the Press, who, like vultures, could scent an unsavoury scandal from a vast distance.

"I don't understand it," said Barbara. "How could he? It's a sin to commit suicide."

"It's a sin to—to have an affair," I rejoined. That, I think, had shocked me more than the suicide.

Meanwhile rumours of more 'affairs' were also circulating among the Brethren all over England and Mr James Taylor was still dominating the horizon from America. Insidiously, new doctrine was being introduced which carried to extremes Mr Darby's original idea of exclusivism founded on 'separation from evil'. Most of the new 'rules', but not all, were based loosely upon isolated verses of the Bible taken completely out of context.

The reason given for the sudden influx of new doctrine, which aimed to 'purify' the Brethren, was that the return of the Lord Jesus in triumph to the earth was imminent. It therefore behoved his 'True Church' to make sure it was ready for his coming. To do this it must be 'purified' and anything 'evil' must be expelled. The most important chapter in the new creed was from St. Paul's second letter to his young assistant, Timothy. It was the one on which Mr Darby had based his 'separation from evil' doctrine: *Let everyone that nameth the name of Christ depart from iniquity.*

That verse had been engraved on my brain from a very early age but Mr Taylor from his ivory tower in New York now decided Mr Darby's policy was not exclusive enough. He homed in on Paul's following confusing instructions about 'vessels' some of which were 'to honour' and some 'to dishonour'. The Brethren apparently were to become 'vessels to honour' and thus would be 'sanctified and serviceable to the Master'.

But any 'vessels to dishonour' were to be immediately cast out so the 'assembly' could be purged of 'iniquity' and would therefore be 'pure' for the return of the Lord. Unfortunately 'iniquity' soon became synonymous with not following to the letter any outrageous new doctrine Mr Taylor and his henchmen might dream up.

Having established this principle, Mr Taylor turned his attention to another of Paul's letters—that to the Corinthian Church. The Corinth of Paul's day was notorious for its loose living encouraged by the many pagan religions. It was understandable, therefore, that the Apostle was concerned to protect his flock from the evil influences surrounding it. He didn't mince his words and instructed his followers 'not even to eat' with anyone who was 'immoral or greedy or worships idols or is a slanderer or a drunkard or a thief'.

The isolating of the words 'with such an one not even to eat' proved the catalyst which was to shake the Exclusive Brethren group to its foundations. Ironically the list that preceded it appeared to be ignored; all Brethren were now forbidden to eat with anyone who wasn't 'Breaking Bread'.

This ban, of course, included those who had been 'withdrawn from' for daring to disagree with this very divisive doctrine. It didn't, at this time, seem to include those who were acting immorally. Apparently you could 'sleep with' someone as long as you didn't 'eat with outsiders'.

The result of this 'purging', therefore, was that many members were either 'withdrawn from' or left of their own accord. Christian love, which had once been so prevalent, had been replaced by hard, implacable authoritarianism. In a system where the infallibility of the leadership was so deeply ingrained, it wasn't difficult for a strong leader to impose his will on a cowed flock.

Sisters, as well as brothers, were now expected to attend Care Meetings. The 'business' of these usually consisted of a stream of 'withdrawals'. Even if an brother had 'withdrawn' himself, it was still necessary for the formal rejection to take place at a Care Meeting—preferably with the individual concerned present.

I attended one such meeting but it was such a terrible ordeal I never went again. Mr Hutton, a gentle brother, for whom I had great respect, was in trouble because his wife's invalid sister, who was not 'in the Meeting', lived with them and had her meals at the same table.

Mr Wickens and others had visited the 'sinner' to try to persuade him of the error of his ways but he saw no reason not to 'eat with' his sister-in-law, who was a committed Christian and attended the local Baptist Church. According to the Brethren, she was not, therefore 'walking in the Light' and Mr Hutton was instructed to appear before the Assembly. If I'd realised what was going to happen, I'd never have gone.

After a hymn and a short prayer Mr Wickens started.

"We are here to discuss the case of our dear brother, Mr Hutton," he boomed. "We are very sad he persists in disobeying Mr Taylor's doctrine based on Paul's first letter to the Corinthians—"

Mr Hutton tried to interrupt. "But the people Paul is referring to are adulterers, robbers, drunkards and so on; surely the Scripture is not meant to … "

"Silence!" roared Mr Wickens. "How dare you try to justify your evil behaviour. You must not eat with anyone who is not 'walking in the Light' and … " His voice became louder and louder as he warmed to his theme while his poor victim kept jumping to his feet and trying to read from the Bible.

But he was given no opportunity to do so. I was horrified. It was the first time the Brethren had really disgusted me. Were they really refusing to listen to words from the Bible they'd always regarded as their one and only guide book?

I took some deep breaths but I didn't think I could cope with much more of this unchristian behaviour and the tears started to flow. It was obvious no one was going to listen to Mr Hutton. His 'withdrawal' was inevitable. Mr Wickens and others continued to shout at him while I and many of the sisters sobbed uncontrollably. Eventually my father, too, had had enough and dragged me out. I cried all the way home and nothing he said could comfort me. My cosy world that had sheltered me all my life had been shattered into a million fragments and nothing would ever be the same again.

That night was one of the most miserable of my life. I couldn't sleep and I prowled round my room pondering all the awful things that were happening. It wasn't right. How could the Brethren behave in such a dreadful way? I felt in such a muddle but through it all I still had the deep sense of knowing Jesus was close to me and he would never change whatever the Brethren did or said. More and more it seemed that what was taking place had nothing to do with him at all.

But life seemed very empty now the 'prop' the Brethren had provided, seemed in danger of slipping from me. I decided I couldn't face the Meeting the following day and my parents went without me.

I staggered into school on the Monday feeling as if I were convalescing after a virulent illness. But I wasn't convalescing; I was still suffering from the 'disease'. It was very hard to concentrate on my work and at lunch time, finding the Ladies Room deserted, I let myself go and indulged in a hearty cry.

Of course it was unlikely I'd be alone for long and soon Barbara came in.

"What on earth's the matter?" she exclaimed.

"Nothing," I sniffed trying to mop up the deluge. "I'm all right. I didn't sleep very well. I'm tired."

"Are you sure that's all it is?" She gave me a concerned look.

Of course it wasn't but I couldn't confide in a Roman Catholic, could I? I still felt some loyalty towards the Brethren although I wasn't quite sure why.

"I wanted to give you this." She held out an envelope.

"What is it?"

"Open it and see."

I did so. "Barbara," I gasped. "I didn't know you were engaged. Congratulations."

"Thanks. We wanted to keep it quiet. But I'd like you to come to the wedding."

I stared at the wedding invitation.

"Oh, Barbara," I wailed. "I can't. I'd love to but … " How could I ever go to a Roman Catholic wedding—or any wedding apart from a Brethren one? I didn't know how to explain but I didn't have to.

"I know," said my friend kindly, handing me her handkerchief to mop up my tears which had started again. "I realise you couldn't be at the Church but you could come to the reception, couldn't you?"

I brightened and then remembered I wasn't allowed to 'eat with' those not 'in the Light'. I sighed. "I'd like to. Can I let you know later?"

"Of course."

I had a lot to think about. It seemed I'd always been a rebel and now I was contemplating flying in the face of Brethren rules. For of course I would go to Barbara's reception. I was touched she'd asked me. If the Brethren discovered what I'd done, that was too bad. I wasn't at all happy with the way things were going and although I'd no plans to desert at the moment, the chances of my remaining with the Brethren for the rest of my life seemed increasingly remote.

The wedding was in July after school had finished for the year and I even made myself a new dress for the occasion; it was doubtful if any of the other guests noticed I hadn't been at the service. Barbara looked lovely in her white veil and I liked her husband who was also a teacher. I enjoyed the reception but the familiar guilt gnomes kept me company.

Meanwhile more and more 'Fellowship Meetings' were being held as Mr Taylor and his followers hurtled round the world enforcing all the new rules. The following September the great man himself took a meeting in Kingston. My parents and I thought we'd better attend although I was very apprehensive. What strange new doctrine might be introduced on our very doorstep? The hall was packed with the faithful and I craned forward to catch a glimpse of Mr Taylor. He seemed far older than when I'd seen him in London and he'd put on weight.

"He looks as though he's ready to drop off to sleep," murmured my father.

I giggled and hastily turned it into a cough. But he was right. Our 'leader' was having trouble keeping his eyes open and his head kept lolling forward. He must be very tired with all the travelling he had to do, I thought tolerantly.

But when he started to speak, it was difficult to follow his train of thought. His unfamiliar accent wasn't the only reason I couldn't understand him. His words were slurred and he kept repeating himself. There were long pauses in the middle of sentences when he peered vaguely round before taking a gulp of water.

Was I being very obtuse? I couldn't understand a word he was saying. I glanced at my parents. My father's lips were compressed and he looked annoyed. My mother was obviously bewildered. Trying to make sense of Mr Taylor's ramblings required too much effort and I floated off into a day dream.

I was brought back abruptly by the announcement of the last hymn and the tea cups rattled as we prepared for the usual tea. But to my surprise, my father stood up.

"We're going home," he announced loudly, glaring at his wife and daughter. He didn't wait to see if we were following but stalked out. By the time we'd collected our belongings, he was half way down the road. I could tell by the way he was walking he was very angry. At last he slowed down so his womenfolk could catch him up.

"What on earth's the matter, Vin?" queried my mother breathlessly. My father rarely became angry so there must be a good reason for his present behaviour.

"Matter?" he roared, towering over us. "The man was as drunk as a lord." And he swept off again.

"Vin!" my mother gasped, scandalized, as she hurried to keep up with him.

I stared after them. Drunk? He couldn't be. It was too preposterous. The Brethren were not teetotal but they didn't get drunk, did they? I'd never seen anyone in that state before but my father had sounded quite convinced. Mr Taylor had certainly been very odd and almost incoherent at times. Whatever had happened to the respectable, clean living, staid brothers I'd been taught to respect?

During the next few months we tried to keep a low profile. Unhappy as I was, it still didn't feel right to leave the Brethren of my own accord. After all they'd originally taken up the 'right' position, hadn't they? And where else would I go? It was very difficult to contemplate the thought of leaving although I thoroughly disagreed with Mr Taylor's unscriptural rules. There was an element of fear too. How could I face being 'withdrawn from' a group that had moulded me, gripped me, taught me and—yes—even cared for me all my life?

Perhaps because I was so miserable, I started to think of moving. Dare I apply for a post overseas? If I could get away from Woking, perhaps things might improve. My father's family had moved to Canada some years earlier and I wondered if I could get a teaching post where at least I would have some link. Of course none of them was 'in the Meeting' so I wouldn't be able to 'eat with them'! I decided to ignore that and apply to a school in Hamilton, Ontario, where I knew there was a Meeting. I was very naïve to think I'd be able to get away with it but the thought of spreading my wings provided a tiny pinprick of light in an otherwise pitch dark tunnel.

I was delighted the Hamilton Board of Education offered me a post in Westdale Collegiate for the following September.

"I want to take it," I told my parents.

"You must do what you feel is best for you," my father said, adding with a grin, "I wish I could come with you."

"We'll miss you," said my mother sadly.

"It'll only be for a year," I said giving her a hug. I felt happier than I'd done for months.

Mr Granger wasn't too pleased when I handed in my notice the next day but he realised I was under considerable pressure and eventually gave me his blessing. I didn't expect the same from the Brethren!

Things had worsened as the attitude of the Woking Brethren hardened towards those 'sinners' who were not toeing the party line. Mr Wickens cornered me one Sunday morning after the Meeting. I felt my breath come in short gasps. Had he heard about my cycling to the town without a hat? Or—horror of horrors—surely I hadn't been seen talking to my Crusader friend, Rosemary, whom I'd met the previous day.

But my misdeameanour was more serious. Mr Wickens gazed solemnly at me. "Are you still going into school assemblies, Marion?" he demanded.

I was taken aback. "Yes, of course," I said without thinking. "I have to."

He shook his head sadly. "No, I don't think you do, Marion. You have the right to withdraw on—er—religious grounds."

It took me a while to find my voice. "You mean like the Muslims, Hindus, Jehovah's Witnesses and Jews?" I queried.

I knew I should have kept my mouth shut. It never did any good to argue with the Brethren.

"Mr Darby states quite clearly we must 'withdraw from evil'." Mr Wickens' monotonous voice pronounced the well worn cliche.

"Surely he wasn't thinking of school assemblies," I said horrified, thinking of the Christian teachers who often led them. "Besides I've been going into them since I was five. I really don't think I could justify my sudden refusal to attend."

My tormenter's thin lips almost disappeared. "I have to tell you, Marion," he announced sternly, "that you will be offending the Brethren if you continue to go into school assemblies."

He stalked off and I glared after him. I wondered how he'd find out whether I'd obeyed him. I certainly had no intention of doing so.

My mother was the next one to be attacked. It was the following Sunday evening and this time it was Mr Pierce who accosted her. He always reminded me of a weasel with his tiny pinprick eyes.

"Ah, Mrs Field, I've been asked, ah …, to, ah …, em—" He came to a stop and I came to my mother's rescue.

"You were saying, Mr Pierce?"

"Ah yes. I believe you, er … work, er … a shop, several days a weeks."

My mother looked as though she wanted to escape but she stood her ground.

"Yes I do."

"But surely you should be at home—er—looking after the children."

My mother looked bewildered. "Both my daughters are grown up, Mr Pierce. I hardly think they need 'looking after'."

I had a mild attack of hysterics and the gentleman suddenly became annoyed. His weasel eyes snapped furiously.

"You shouldn't be out at work," he hissed. "A woman's place is in the home and as for your younger daughter, she should be at home too. Mr Taylor has said young people must not leave home until they marry."

The Brethren had always looked askance at married sisters who chose to work but the ban on leaving home was quite new. It was the first I'd heard of this latest edict. Fortunately my father suddenly appeared to rescue his beleaguered wife. He'd obviously heard Mr Pierce's last speech and was not pleased.

"I don't require your assistance in the running of my household, Mr Pierce," he snapped. "What my wife and daughters do is no concern of yours." He marched us off, still fuming.

"Oh dear," gasped my mother. "I don't think you should have said that, Vin. You know how awkward they can be."

My father stopped. "You don't want to give up work, do you?" he demanded.

"You know I don't." My mother had worked in one of the local drapers for many years. She'd originally trained as a window dresser and took great pride in her work.

"Well they're not going to dictate to us."

My mother sighed as we started off again. "They will though, won't they?" she said sadly. "I don't think I can take much more of this awful atmosphere."

"What's this about young people not leaving home till they're married?" I suddenly enquired. "I haven't heard that before."

"It came out in one of the recent London Meetings. It's worse than that, though. Apparently higher education is no longer allowed and all students are supposed to leave College and return home."

"Oh my goodness." The implications of this took some while to assimilate. "That means there won't be any teachers, doctors, nurses, lawyers, dentists ... "

"All right, all right," interrupted my father testily. "You don't need to list them all. I'm more worried about Meriel."

For the moment I'd forgotten my sister. She was now in her second year in Bristol. She would be in trouble on two counts; she was in higher education and she was living away from home.

"Why didn't you tell me about it?" wailed my mother. "What are you going to do about her?"

"I didn't want to worry you and I don't want to talk about it now. I've got to think about it."

He spent the whole of the next week thinking. It was almost impossible to get him to talk at all. In the evenings he sat in the garden frowning into space.

"I do wish he'd tell us what he's going to do," worried my mother one evening as we did the washing up. "All this uncertainty is so unsettling."

"I'm sure he'll sort something out," I replied trying to convince myself that somehow he'd be able to return us to the status quo. He couldn't, of course. Things had gone too far and there was no going back. The next night after supper he broke his self imposed silence.

"I've got something to tell you," he announced. "I've decided that, as head of the household, I'd better 'withdraw' myself from the Brethren. Then that will make it easier for you both—and Meriel. I'm the one who's always been the black sheep. If I go, you can probably stay on."

"Don't be ridiculous," scoffed my mother. "If you go, I'm going with you. You don't think I'm going to have you eating your meals alone in the kitchen do you?"

He looked startled. For an intelligent man, it didn't seem to me he'd thought things out very carefully.

"Of course Mummy's right," I assured him. "If you go, we'll all go. You don't think I want to stay in those circumstances, do you? They probably wouldn't have me anyway."

My father shook his head. "No, Marion, I don't think you should leave at the moment. I do realise you probably won't last long either but please don't go now."

I struggled with my feelings. My father was right, of course. I was hoping to avoid a confrontation but I would have to come to my own decision. It wasn't fair to rely on him this time.

"All right," I agreed at last reluctantly. "But I expect I'll follow you soon. So how are you going to do it?"

"I've written a letter to the Brethren saying I can't go on with them because of all the unscriptural doctrine they're following and because of the lack of love they're showing to any who disagree with them."

"They don't seem at all like the Brethren we used to know, do they?" I said sadly. "They used to be so caring. Now they're so hard."

My mother suddenly burst into tears. "Oh don't do that, dear," pleaded my father. He hated tears. "Do you really mind so much?"

"No, it's just that it, … it seems so sad after all this time."

"I know but the Lord Jesus doesn't change, does he? He's still the same."

"He must be very hurt by what's going on," I said, searching for my own handkerchief.

My mother dried her eyes. "I'm sure it's for the best, Vin. We couldn't go on like this."

"What about Meriel?"

"She's under age so she'll have to do as I say. She'll stay on at College and complete her three years."

Neither of my parents attended the Meeting on the following Sunday so I went alone although I no longer felt part of the proceedings. Although the service was, as usual, the Lord's Supper, some of the 'prayers'—if such they could be called—were a tirade against 'those of our number who have turned from the Light'.

I felt extremely uncomfortable and was made even more so, when, after the Meeting was over and there was the usual shuffling of feet, Mr Wickens stood up, cleared his throat and announced in funereal tones, "I have received a letter from our dear brother, Mr Field, which I should like to read."

I hadn't seen the letter and shouldn't have been surprised at my father's rhetoric. He'd always had a gift with words and I couldn't have put it better myself. I was proud of him.

When Mr Wickens had finished, he announced there would be a Care Meeting the following Saturday to discuss it. I left as quickly as I could. No one wanted to speak to me although I received several sympathetic glances. I'd had enough. It was the last meeting of the Exclusive Brethren I ever attended.

Of course I wasn't allowed to escape without a visit from Mr Wickens and Mr Pierce. I was determined not to get drawn into any arguments. The Brethren were adept at trapping their victims in nets of their own making.

It was two weeks after my parents had been 'withdrawn from' that I had my visitation. My parents went out on the Saturday afternoon and my grandmother rested in her room while I prepared to receive my visitors. I took some deep breaths to calm myself as I stared round our spacious drawing room. My love of the dramatic, smothered for so long, wriggled to the surface and I determined to 'set the scene' so I should be in the dominant position.

I moved the high piano stool to a strategic position facing the two deep arm chairs. My inquisitors would have great difficulty in getting out of them with any dignity, I thought gleefully. The forthcoming interview seemed to have little to do with Christianity whose leader had been gentle and caring but who had also shown anger at injustice and hypocrisy. I said a quick prayer asking for calmness and tolerance. Because the Brethren had become so ruthless and unchristian, it didn't mean I had to retaliate in kind.

The doorbell interrupted my musings and, after a quick glance at my 'set', I swept to the door.

"Good afternoon. Do come in," I said giving a creditable imitation of a gracious hostess.

"Thank you."

I relieved them of their hats which they were, of course, wearing, even on this hot July day.

"Do sit down." I gestured towards the two arm chairs and watched them sink inexorably down. I sat on the piano stool and imagined I was Oscar Wilde's Lady Bracknell looking haughtily down her nose at two unwelcome visitors. I straightened my back, folded my hands in my lap and waited.

The silence seemed interminable. I wondered if this was a new tactic designed to wear down recalcitrant sisters. But I was certainly not going to break it. At last Mr Wickens decided to do so.

"You know your parents have now been 'withdrawn from'."

"Yes."

"They are very wicked to have turned their backs on the Light. You realise that, don't you, Marion?"

I glared at him, my impersonation of Lady Bracknell improving by the minute.

"You really expect me to say my parents are wicked?" I demanded in horrified hauteur.

They glanced uneasily at each other.

"Yes," snapped Mr Pierce.

"Well I won't." Lady Bracknell disappeared and I reverted to my childhood behaviour when I was told to do something to which I objected.

Mr Wickens shook his head reprovingly. "I trust you don't still eat with your parents, Marion."

I was still revelling in my childhood role. "Of course I do. They wouldn't let me eat on my own in the kitchen."

"You could have a tray and then you wouldn't be sitting at the same table," suggested Mr Pierce.

I stared at him, my anger briefly replaced by an irrepressible urge to giggle which I hastily suppressed. Fortunately Mr Pierce didn't seem to expect an answer and they apparently decided they'd won round one. Mr Wickens weighed in for round two.

"You're not still going into school assemblies, are you?" he barked.

I thought this was a rhetorical question as I'd already told him my views on that subject but he was waiting for an answer. Reinstating Lady Bracknell, I informed him again that, as I'd been attending school assemblies since I'd first gone to school, I saw no reason to stop now, particularly as I'd be leaving my present school at the end of the month.

That provided the opening for round three. "Ah yes. We understand you are going to move away from home."

I found their obvious disapproval puzzling. As my parents had been 'withdrawn from', surely they should be delighted to hear I was going to be removed from their influence.

"Yes, I'm going to Canada," I announced baldly.

This gave Mr Wickens the opportunity to move in for the kill.

"You realise we won't be able to give you a 'letter of commendation'."

"Yes." I didn't want one!

"So you are prepared to turn your back on 'the Light' with all that entails."

I nodded.

"I'm afraid she'll find life very difficult," murmured Mr Pierce.

Mr Wickens nodded. "A young girl on her own is open to all kinds of temptations." They seemed to have forgotten I was there. But I understood their implications and Lady Bracknell swept back to dominate the last stages of the conflict.

"I assure you, gentlemen," I said between clenched teeth, "I have no intention of forgetting the high moral standards I've been set by my parents."

"So you're quite determined to go to Canada." Mr Wickens sounded resigned.

"Yes."

He gazed mournfully at me. "I'm sure you'll be very miserable," he said.

"Thank you very much."

Lady Bracknell swept to her feet and haughtily ushered her visitors out. Once they'd gone, I returned to the drawing room and collapsed on the sofa. My back hurt from my enforced ramrod posture and now the adrenaline was no longer flowing, I was exhausted. I felt numb too. I was free—free from the strait jacket that had confined me all my life. At last I'd broken those iron fetters that had bound me and I could take my first tentative steps into a 'world' where many other Christians had always lived without being 'contaminated'. I couldn't believe it yet. Of course I would have to be formally 'withdrawn from' at the next Care Meeting but I had no intention of going to it.

My grandmother was the next to incur the wrath of the Brethren. She was very distressed by their current activities and it wasn't long before she, too, was on their black list. Mrs Wickens and Mrs Pierce came to visit her when they knew she'd be alone—an unkind thing to do. However, when she regaled us with an account of the visit, it was obvious she'd managed to stay in control.

She'd also been expected to say her daughter and son-in-law were 'wicked' and she wouldn't eat with them any more.

"I said you didn't fit into any of the categories St. Paul mentions in his letter," she told us. "I even asked them if they could support what they said from the Bible. They couldn't, of course. They kept on and on at me about how wrong it was for me to eat with you and in the end I'd had enough. I reminded them I was an old lady and warned them if they didn't go, I'd probably have a heart attack. They couldn't get out of the house fast enough," she ended gleefully.

My father chuckled. "I wish I'd been a fly on the wall."

"I don't think it's funny, Vin," said my mother crossly. "They'd no right to treat mother like that."

"I don't want to see anyone else," my grandmother announced. "I'm going to write them a letter."

A few days later there was a knock at the door about nine o'clock in the evening. I dragged myself away from my book and went to open it. Mr Wickens and Mr Pierce stood there.

"We wish to see Mrs Coombs," stated Mr Wickens.

"She's in bed," I told them.

"We have a right to see her on Assembly business."

"She's probably asleep. You can't expect an old lady to receive visitors at this time of night."

"Please tell her we're here."

I debated whether to shut the door in their faces but decided against it. I left them and tiptoed into my grandmother's room. Her light was on and she was reading.

"Mr Wickens and Mr Pierce have come to see you, Grandma. I told them you were in bed and probably asleep. You don't want to see them, do you?"

"Certainly not. They've upset me enough already. Tell them my letter is final and I don't want any more to do with them."

I relayed the message.

"Her case will come up at the Care Meeting on Saturday," intoned Mr Wickens. "We will send a car for her. Please inform her we shall expect her to be there."

I slammed the door before I could say anything I'd regret. My grandmother hadn't gone out in the evening for months. She said the dark made her feel giddy and she certainly wouldn't want to go to a Meeting merely to hear a catalogue of all her misdeeds.

Other families were also having problems, among them the Huttons. They had a twenty year old daughter, Jennifer. Unlike me, she'd opted to stay with the Brethren. Eventually, merely 'not eating with' her parents was considered insufficient. She was instructed to cut herself off completely from them. To enable her to do this she had to leave her home and move in with the Pierces who lived opposite the Huttons. To my amazement, I heard Jennifer had agreed.

"Poor Mrs Hutton," said my mother with tears in her eyes. "Fancy seeing Jennifer going to work every day but not being able to speak to her. It does seem so wicked."

It also seemed illogical considering what I'd been told. But worse was to come. The Pierces had a son and the next thing we heard was that Jennifer and Paul were to be married. One evening the phone rang and my mother answered it. She was talking for a long time and when she came back, she was obviously upset.

"That was Mrs Hutton," she said. "Poor woman. I feel so sorry for her. Jennifer and Paul are to be married next Saturday. Mr and Mrs Hutton thought they'd at least be able to go to the Registry Office and the Wedding Meeting even if they avoided the Reception. But Jennifer's just phoned to tell them not to go at all. She says it will be too embarrassing and her Uncle, Mr Hutton's brother, will take the place of her father. How could she be so cruel?" My mother was almost crying herself.

We invited Mr and Mrs Hutton to spend their daughter's wedding day with us, but, not surprisingly, it wasn't a happy occasion. Mrs.Hutton cried all the time and there was nothing we could say to comfort her.

There were other similar incidents and there were other tragedies too. One brilliant young brother in his third year at Oxford tried to take his own life rather than be forced to leave University. There were other suicides and mental breakdowns as the 'exclusive laws' were tightened still further and more families were divided. Working with 'outsiders' was banned and brothers were forced to give up lucrative jobs and either start up their own businesses or work for other Brethren.

I was relieved my forthcoming trip to Canada would take my mind off the trauma of the last few months. But there was one shadow still hovering over my family. My sister was still with the Brethren. The Meeting in Bristol didn't appear to be taking quite such a hard line as Woking, and Meriel, while agreeing to stay on at College as my father wished, didn't want to 'withdraw from' the Brethren. However, when she came home for the summer holidays, she behaved just as she had always done towards us although my parents agreed she could have her meals on a tray so she wasn't 'eating with us'!

I'd been in the throes of preparation for my big adventure for the past few weeks. I only intended to stay in Canada for a year but after five years' teaching in England, I couldn't afford a return ticket. I hoped my Canadian salary would be an improvement. I was to stay with relatives in Toronto until I found accommodation in Hamilton.

My parents and sister came with me to London to wave me off on the train to Liverpool from where I was to board the *Carinthia* to sail across the Atlantic.

It was to be ten years before I saw my sister again.

Chapter Ten

Canada

It didn't take long to adjust to life on board ship. I loved dressing up for dinner and wearing the long evening gown I'd bought for the Captain's cocktail party. After dinner, there was dancing and I even indulged in that. Fortunately my partners were usually the ship's officers who were obviously adept at steering partners with two left feet!

I was glad I had five days in which to adjust to my new status; no one on board knew anything about my background and I was determined it would stay that way. When we arrived in Montreal, I boarded the train to go to Toronto where I was to be met.

I soon started to wonder how I was going to recognise my relatives. I hadn't a photograph and I'd never thought to send them one! When I arrived, the station was flooded with people. It would be like looking for a needle in a haystack, I thought in despair. But at least the language all around me was English and I had a tongue in my head.

But I needn't have worried. Suddenly, above the cacophony of sound, a voice boomed out.

"Marion Field. Marion Field."

I looked round and at last located the owner of the trumpet. It was a tiny old lady frantically waving around a handbag almost as large as she was. Pushing my luggage trolley, I staggered towards her and was immediately enfolded in a tight embrace.

"This is Doris," she shouted, releasing me and squinting up at a large beaming lady who stood beside her.

I smiled back. "Hullo, Doris. It's lovely to see you and it's so kind of you to have me to stay."

"We're glad to have you, aren't we, Mother?" Already I was getting used to the soft Canadian accent.

Aunt Flo eyed my luggage disapprovingly. "Is that all yours?" she demanded in disbelief. "I don't know where you're going to put it all."

"Don't worry, Mother. We'll find room. Come on." Doris wheeled off my laden trolley and I followed her through the crowds to her car where I started to get into the driving seat.

She looked at me with a grin. "Going to drive, are you?"

I blushed. "Sorry. I forgot you drive on the right."

"You'll soon get used to it."

I sat in the back while Aunt Flo clambered into the front and we were off. Everything seemed so huge compared with England. The cars were bigger, the roads wider and even the buildings towered high above us. Sitting with my nose glued to the window, I absorbed the view flashing past.

The journey was short and then we were home. It was pleasant to be in a house again after travelling for several days and I was looking forward to relaxing for a while before starting work. But I'd reckoned without Doris. She was thrilled to have an English cousin staying with her and she was determined not to waste any time. As I'd spent most of my life being told what to do and what not to do, I was quite happy to let her organise my life for me.

The following day was Sunday and I went with her to the Church she attended—an Anglican one. It obviously hadn't occurred to her I might have preferred a nonconformist Church. To attend an Anglican Church service only a few weeks after leaving the Exclusive Brethren seemed rather a drastic step to take. As I sat in the pew, I tried to look as if I did this every week. It was soon quite clear I didn't! I couldn't find my way round the Prayer Book and I had to keep a surreptitious eye on Doris so I knew when to kneel, when to stand and when to sit. I was so busy making sure I was doing the right thing, there wasn't much time left to concentrate on what was being said!

When I did realise what was going on, I discovered, to my horror, it was a Communion Service. I sat there, coiled in embarrassment as the preacher ascended the pulpit to preach. Now, I thought anxiously, we shall hear the heresies the Brethren were always talking about. I concentrated hard but to my amazement, I didn't hear anything that wasn't related to the Bible. I glanced round me. The sun shone through the stained glass windows and candles sparkled on the altar, above which was a large wooden cross. I pursed my lips. Surely these trappings were not necessary, I thought. The Brethren had always said any decoration detracted from the service.

The preacher came down from the pulpit and the service continued. Soon people started to shuffle into the aisle so they could go up to the altar to receive Communion. I noticed one or two people were still sitting in their places so I didn't feel too conspicuous. There was no way I could have taken Communion in an Anglican Church so soon after leaving a totally different way of worshipping. I shook my head as Doris stood up and clambered past me.

I thought about my future. I didn't think I could join an Anglican Church. It was too 'high' and I wasn't used to a set pattern of service. I'd have to wait and see what Churches there were in Hamilton.

The following week Doris drove me there and we stopped in front of the school where I was to teach.

"That's a school!" I exclaimed in amazement. "It looks more like a prison."

It was a vast stone building with three storeys and the windows seemed to be barred. Playing fields surrounded it and I assumed I'd be using these until the weather became too bad.

"How many students do you think there are?" I asked Doris apprehensively.

"About two thousand I should think. That's the usual number for a Canadian High School."

"Wow!" The largest school I'd taught in so far had been six hundred.

"They start High School at thirteen here, you know," my cousin informed me. "And they stay till eighteen usually."

"Mm." I was terrified already. What on earth was I doing here? Why hadn't I stayed at home?

Doris started the car again. "We'd better find somewhere for you to live. I've got some addresses."

We only went to one. It was only two streets away from the school so I should be able to walk even in the bad weather. I liked Mrs Percival on sight and she seemed to approve of me. She showed me the bedsitter I could have. Fortunately it was large enough to absorb all my belongings.

"If you like, I can cook you an evening meal. Or you might prefer to cook for yourself?"

"It would be lovely to have an evening meal. Thank you."

I moved in the following day and Doris helped me unpack and arrange my things. I was sorry to say goodbye to her. She seemed a bridge between my old and new lives but Mrs Percival was determined to make me feel at home.

"I've just made a pot of tea," she announced as I returned to the house after waiting till my cousin's car had disappeared round the corner. "Would you like one?"

"Oh yes, please." I followed her into the kitchen while she poured the tea.

"There's a quiz programme on the television I usually watch. Do you like television? I expect you have different programmes in England, don't you?"

I was taken by surprise and for a moment I couldn't think of any reply to such a very ordinary question. She looked puzzled and I hastily covered up my embarrassment with a half truth.

"I ... I haven't watched very much recently. But please do watch the quiz programme. I should like to see it."

She switched it on and I luxuriated in my first evening of television. I couldn't think why the Brethren had made such a fuss about it. I enjoyed the quiz programme and then we watched the news. I was quite sorry to have to tear myself away to prepare for school the following day.

I didn't sleep much that night but the next day when I entered the vast building, I still thought of as 'the prison', I found all the inhabitants very friendly. I liked Jan, the Head of the Physical Education Department where I was to work and she gave me detailed instructions about what I should be doing. It seemed much more formal than I was used to and the students had examinations at the end of each term.

The following day I met some of them and after their initial reaction to my 'limey' accent, we got on well together although I hadn't expected to have to teach basketball and volleyball, neither of which I knew anything about! I got my own back by introducing hockey! One evening I took the Department to the local park with the hockey sticks and ball we'd found in the back of one of the cupboards.

It wasn't long before we collected a bewildered crowd round us including a policeman. Eventually his curiosity got the better of him and cornering me as I was chasing the ball, he demanded, "What are you doing?"

"We're playing hockey," I gasped.

"Hockey!" he scoffed. "That's played on ice."

"She means 'field hockey'," explained Jan rescuing me. "You don't mind, do you, Officer? Perhaps you'd be kind enough to move these people away. They might get hurt."

Shaking his head and muttering to himself, he moved towards the grinning crowd who weren't pleased to have their evening's entertainment curtailed.

Mrs Percival, I'd discovered, belonged to the Salvation Army and when she suggested I might like to attend a service with her, I agreed. Why not? I might as well sample as many different types of service as I could before I finally made my choice. So the following Sunday I accompanied my landlady to a service unlike any I could ever have imagined. Formality was conspicuous by its absence and while used to a certain amount of freedom in worship, this seemed to go to extremes and I was quite bewildered.

The Brethren had had no musical accompaniments but the Salvation Army, of course, was famous for its music so I'd expected the usual band. But I was rather startled when some of the females in the congregation suddenly leapt to their feet waving percussion instruments as they danced around the room. I felt even more embarrassed than I had the Previous Sunday. Surely this wasn't a very reverent way to behave. I didn't think the Brethren would have approved at all.

But I mustn't think of them. I'd left them and I must try to forget they were always right. They hadn't been right at all latterly, I reminded myself. There were after all other ways of doing things and the musicians leaping enthusiastically around me looked much happier than the Brethren had usually looked. They seemed to feel the words they were singing too. I was starting to wonder why it was the Brethren had always insisted their way was the only one. Compared to the rest of Christendom, they were a very small group. I was discovering there were a vast number of Christians who weren't Brethren.

However, I didn't think the Salvation Army would provide me with my spiritual home. The Anglican was too formal and the Salvation Army too informal. I'd have to find something in between.

This 'something' proved to be St. Cuthbert's Presbyterian Church which was very near my lodgings. So the next Sunday I put on the hat I still felt I had to wear to Church and for the first time went alone to a new Church. I was delighted to be given a warm welcome and before long, I knew this was where I should worship during my time in Canada.

I even joined the choir and was relieved to find that, as well as the purple gowns, the lady members wore mortar boards on their heads. I thoroughly enjoyed the weekly rehearsals and was delighted when I was asked to sing a solo. I consoled myself with the thought that I wasn't 'speaking' in the 'assembly', only singing. I doubt if the Brethren would have appreciated the difference!

As I'd found in both the Anglican service and the Salvation Army, the preaching was firmly based on the Bible. I still hadn't heard any of the heresy that the Brethren had always insisted was such a feature of all other Churches. How arrogant they were to think they, and only they, had the 'Truth'.

But I was surprised when I discovered the Presbyterian church only held a Communion Service once a month. In the Brethren I had, of course, 'Broken Bread' every Sunday. However this gave me time to adapt to the trauma of taking the Lord's Supper in a different setting for the first time. It seemed right to do so and, having regaled the Minister, Mr Aldridge, with the story of my past, I was relieved he agreed.

In the Service I was startled by the use of individual cups for the wine instead of a single cup. I recognised this was more hygienic but somehow it didn't seem quite right. Neither did the use of grape juice instead of wine. However, having checked my Bible, I discovered the words used in one Gospel were 'the fruit of the vine'. That, I decided, meant grape juice as well as wine.

After I'd been attending the Church for some time, I asked the Sunday School Superintendent if I could teach a Sunday School class. As I was a qualified teacher, I thought he'd be delighted to be able to use me. How wrong I was!

"I think we've got enough teachers at the moment. And, of course, I'd have to check with Mr Aldridge before I could use you."

"Of course," I echoed, my self-esteem receiving a jolt. I knew it wasn't easy to get teachers for the Sunday School; and qualified teachers were rarely willing to offer their professional services on Sunday after teaching all week. So what was wrong with me?

I was soon given the answer. Mr Aldridge waylaid me after an evening service.

"I hear you've offered to help in the Sunday School," he said.

"Yes, but Mr Patrick doesn't seem very keen."

"I think you'll find he can find a place for you." He grinned at me. "I've assured him you won't teach the children any heresy."

"What?" I gasped, outraged.

Mr Aldridge hastened to smooth my ruffled feathers. "He didn't know much about you, you see. He had to be sure your teaching would be based firmly on the Bible."

I nodded, my annoyance gone. How ironic that I, who'd been brought up to believe all other Churches were preaching heresy, should be suspected of the same thing. It was a sobering thought. But I was glad the misunderstanding had been cleared up and I enjoyed teaching the teenagers before the morning Service.

Apart from my Church and school activities, I also joined the Bach-Elgar choir which met every week. I was thrilled at last to be able to put my love of singing to good use. There were over a hundred members and I was delighted to hear we'd be singing Handel's *Messiah* just before Christmas. I'd always resented the lack of music in the Brethren and could never understand why they disapproved of sacred music even when the words were taken directly from the Bible as in the case of the *Messiah*.

Of course, they'd used hymns but they'd sometimes changed the words. My father had always been very irritated by the use of the word 'praise' which the Brethren had substituted for 'love' in the famous hymn *Love divine, all loves excelling*. I agreed that 'Love divine, all praise excelling' didn't really make sense! I'd always been puzzled too by Mr Darby's preface to the 1881 edition of the hymn book, where he suggested hymns should contain 'something at least of the spirit of poetry, though not poetry itself, which is objectionable, as merely the spirit and imagination of man'.

I wondered if he'd have felt the same about the music of Handel's Oratorio. I found it extremely moving and was impressed by the way in which the Scriptures had been used to produce orally the story of God's dealing with man, both in the past and in the future. I could quite believe the composer had seen angels while he was writing the stirring *Hallelujah Chorus*. I sang my heart out at rehearsals and had usually lost my voice by the time I went home.

As the time for the performance drew near, a long cream evening dress was made for me. All the female members of the choir wore identical dresses so they were all made to measure. So once again, I was able to indulge my love of 'dressing up'—even if I did look the same as everyone else!

At the last rehearsal, we were given final instructions. "Don't forget, ladies," said the secretary of the society, "that we'll be under lights; wear make up so your faces can be seen. The audience won't want to look at a white blur of faces."

It was taking me a long time to formulate my new 'image'. It was only a few months since I'd left the Brethren and old habits die hard! I hadn't any idea what make up to buy. I was too proud to confess my ignorance to any of my new friends so the next day I went into the town and hesitantly approached one of the cosmetic counters in one of the large department stores. The salesgirl was beautifully made up so I hoped she'd be able to give me some advice.

She smiled at me. "Can I help you, ma'am?"

I smiled back. "I hope so. I'm afraid I'm a complete novice at the art of make up and I'm singing in a concert next week. We'll be under lights and have been told to wear enough make up to be seen. I never wear it and I really don't know what to buy. Can you advise me, please."

"Of course. I'll be delighted to. Now let me see." Her professional eye roamed over the countenance of this strange being whose face had remained just as nature intended. I think she was enjoying the challenge.

"I think this is the right colour for your foundation and you'll need a blusher for your cheeks. Brush it on to your cheekbones and up towards your eyes—like this." She demonstrated. "Now you need an eyebrow pencil and some mascara—light brown I think and a highlighter for just below your eyebrows." She burrowed under the counter and after producing the items, gave me another penetrating stare. "I think you should wear green eyeshadow. You've got green flecks in your eyes. Oh, you'd better take this, too. It's make up remover."

"Thank you. Is there anything else I need?"

"No, that should be all right. I hope you enjoy using it. I should have a practice before you go out wearing it."

"Oh, I will."

Later, in my bedroom, I excitedly experimented with my new purchases. I was glad I was alone as my first attempts made me resemble Coco the clown rather than a prospective chorister. I couldn't even smooth the foundation cream evenly over my face. I looked as though I hadn't washed for days. However, fortunately practice made—almost perfect.

I was flattered by the compliments I received when I arrived for the concert.

"You look beautiful," exclaimed one of my fellow songsters. "My goodness, doesn't make up make a difference."

I smiled graciously although it seemed rather a back handed compliment. As we filed out to take our places in front of the vast audience, I experienced a thrill that only a year ago would have seemed impossible. It didn't take me long to acquire a taste for 'performing'. But when the music started, I forgot the audience and revelled in the inspiring music. Never having been to a concert before, I was startled when, at the first chords of the *Hallelujah Chorus*, the audience rose to its feet and stood until the music swelled to its conclusion. I could hardly sing for emotion and I felt very sorry for the soprano soloist who had to follow the stirring sounds. It was a memorable evening.

Two days later term ended and I left to spend Christmas with an uncle and aunt who lived in Albany, the capital of New York State. I was looking forward to crossing the border but I was slightly apprehensive about the religious aspect of my visit. My uncle was the Priest of an Episcopalian Church and I knew it would be very different from the Presbyterian Service I'd become used to and light years away from Brethren Meetings.

My apprehension grew when my aunt asked if I'd like to go to Midnight Mass on Christmas Eve. My uncle, of course, would be leading the service. The term 'Mass' conjured up horrifying visions of Roman Catholicism which was considered by the Brethren to be the ultimate in heresy. But this would be an Episcopalian Service similar to an Anglican one.

"I'd love to come with you, Aunt Muriel," I replied trying to sound enthusiastic.

"You don't have to if you'd rather not," she said gently.

"I'd like to—really."

We walked through the crisp snow with the stars twinkling above us and the glittering decorations on all the houses lighting our way. I was determined to keep an open mind about the service but it wasn't easy and horror filled me as we passed through the Church door and I almost choked on the pungent smell of incense that wafted towards me. Candles gleamed at the ends of the crowded pews as we moved down towards some seats at the front.

I hardly recognised my uncle in the richly clothed figure making his stately way up the aisle. I felt overawed in the presence of all this splendour.

As the service proceeded, I began to feel more and more uncomfortable. Bells were rung, more incense swirled round, the Priest's headgear was changed and I felt like a Jack in the box as I tried to keep up with my aunt as she stood, sat, knelt and even bowed. I was sure I'd never become used to this type of service and although the sense of reverence was almost tangible, it seemed so far away from that primitive scene in the manger we were celebrating.

I didn't take Communion and I don't think my aunt was surprised. I thought I'd kept my feelings well under control but apparently I hadn't hidden them well enough. When my uncle had gone to bed, my aunt and I sat sipping coffee at the kitchen table. There was an awkward silence and I knew my aunt wanted to say something to me. She seemed to be searching for the right words.

At last she said, "You didn't like the Service very much did you, dear?"

I blushed. I'd hoped she hadn't noticed. "Well, er, it was, er, very different from what I've been used to," I said, lamely.

"Yes dear, I know. You looked quite horrified some of the time."

"Oh dear. I …, I didn't mean to."

She put her coffee cup gently back on the saucer and leaned towards me. "Let me give you some advice, dear. I know you come from a very different background from mine and you've been used to a much more simple service. But I was brought up in a similar Church to the one we went to tonight. Now I know you were puzzled and perhaps even a little repelled by a lot of the ritual. But every single thing that was done has its roots in tradition and in the Bible. To me, it all had a deep significance. You see, dear, we might worship in different ways but we all serve the same God and I'm sure he recognises we're all different and don't always want to do things in the same way. So perhaps you could try to be a little more tolerant too."

I felt ashamed. How right she was. I'd learned a lesson I'd never forget.

When I returned home, I found another piece of my ecumenical jigsaw waiting to be slotted into place. There was a letter from my father. It contained some startling news.

"We've started going regularly to St. Mary of Bethany," he wrote. "We've visited several of the local nonconformist Churches and Chapels but your mother and I both feel the Church of England is now our spiritual home."

"My goodness," I squeaked, struggling to take this in. My parents had actually joined the 'heretical' Anglican Church with its 'clerical system', 'set form of worship' and 'written prayers'. What were they thinking of? I read on.

"As you know, I've always considered the doctrine of the Church of England to be closer to the Brethren than any other. The Creed which is said every Sunday sets out the basic Christian beliefs which, of course, the Brethren always held. What a pity they didn't use a creed. We might all have been spared a lot of heartache though I, for one, am quite relieved to be free of such a rigid system."

He was probably right but it seemed a very big jump to me. One of the criticisms levelled at the Anglicans was that their pattern of worship was 'set' and the prayers written down. But I had to admit that, towards the end, the Brethren pattern was just as rigid and anyone who deviated from it was automatically 'out'.

There was other news in the letter too. My sister was still Breaking Bread and had given up her College course. She was now married to a young brother she'd met in Bristol. The letter had taken some time to reach me and my father told me she was expecting her first child. "I do hope we'll be able to visit her when the baby's born," he wrote. "But I know it's very difficult for her. Roger works on one of the farms belonging to a local brother so obviously they have to keep in line."

I stared out of the window, tears blurring my eyes. I knew how my father loved children. He'd be heartbroken if he couldn't see his grandchild and so would my mother. I was sad for myself too. It would have been lovely to be an aunt. But my sadness was for my sister too. We'd been such a close family and I was sure she must be upset about not being able to see her family. When I'd first arrived in Canada, she'd written me normal sisterly letters but I hadn't heard from her for some time. I put my father's letter away and tried to forget the unhappiness that was still prevalent in so many families because of Mr Taylor's dictates.

During the Easter holidays I was invited to visit yet another cousin, this time in Ohio. Lily introduced me to rural America and by the end of my stay I was quite bemused by all the places I'd seen. But one in particular was to leave a lasting impression. We visited an Amish settlement and I wondered why the Brethren, too, hadn't thought of settling their own little corner of the country as this gentle, friendly group had done. They had literally 'withdrawn from the world'.

I was fascinated as we walked round the settlement. Lily told me the Amish were farmers who produced everything they needed to exist. They were totally self sufficient and no 'outsiders' were permitted to live in the village.

"How did they originate?" I asked Lily as we drew near the village.

"They settled here during the eighteenth century. They broke away from the Mennonites because they thought they were too worldly. They take the Bible literally and follow very strict rules."

"Just like the Brethren," I thought. They, too, had tried to 'withdraw from the world' but had caused a lot of harm by doing so. The Amish people who ambled about their daily business looked serene and happy.

"What happens if someone doesn't agree with something or breaks the rules?" I enquired.

"They're excommunicated and their family will refuse to eat with them."

"Good gracious!" I exclaimed.

"It doesn't sound very Christian, does it?" said Lily, misinterpreting my reaction. "I can't understand anyone behaving like that, can you?"

Oh yes, I could understand only too well but it was not the time to explain the Amish weren't the only group to treat 'sinners' in this way. There was certainly 'nothing new under the sun', I reflected.

"Why are they dressed so oddly?" I asked, intrigued, as an attractive girl passed us, her black skirt sweeping the ground. Her face under its black bonnet was devoid of make up and wore an expression of complete serenity.

"They still wear similar clothes to their ancestors. They're not even allowed to use buttons which were considered too decorative in the eighteenth century so everything has to be tied."

"How strange," I murmured as a black wagon rumbled past driven by a long haired, bearded man dressed entirely in black. On his head he wore a wide-brimmed black hat while a number of little bonnets could be seen bobbing up and down at the back.

"They never use cars," Lily informed me forestalling my next question. "They don't approve of anything mechanical and they don't have telephones or electricity. It must be a strange life but I suppose they're brought up to it and don't know any different."

Just as I'd been, I thought. "I haven't seen any Churches. Where do they worship?"

"In their houses. They elect their ministers by drawing lots and they never have any musical instruments."

More and more like the Brethren, I thought, although we were allowed pianos in our homes and we did have telephones and electricity—thank goodness!

I certainly hadn't expected to find a carbon copy of the Brethren in this corner of the United States of America. It was a shock to discover that 'Exclusivism' was not unique but had actually been put into even more rigid practice as far back as the eighteenth century.

By time I left Canada, I'd started to put the Brethren and my experience of them into some sort of perspective but it would be a long time before I finally came to terms with my background.

I stayed in Ontario for four years instead of the expected one but during my last year I grew restless. Africa had always beckoned me and now I was no longer bound by having to find an Exclusive Meeting, I decided to see if I could fulfil my childhood ambition of being a missionary.

I wrote to a friend who was headmistress of a school in Uganda asking if she had any vacancies. When she replied, I was disappointed to learn that, although she and most of her staff were still missionaries, the school had recently been taken over by the government. However, she wrote, "There's an English post vacant at the moment and I'd love to have you so I suggest you apply to the Ministry of Overseas Development in London as they now appoint 'Education Officers' to Ugandan schools."

I did so; they replied promptly and I was offered an interview at the end of July. I again went home by boat but I felt much more confident than I'd done on my previous trip and I certainly looked different. My hair had gradually become shorter and I was now adept at applying make up.

Nevertheless, I was slightly embarrassed when my parents didn't recognise me!

Chapter Eleven

The Pearl Of Africa

I hardly had time to draw breath after my arrival home before I had to hurtle up to London for my interview at the Ministry of Overseas Development. Clattering down the long corridor in my high heels, I reflected I hadn't had time to feel nervous until then. But sitting outside the unwelcoming wooden door, I allowed the butterflies free rein in my stomach.

Eventually the door was flung open and I was ushered in. Behind the long table sat three solemn gentlemen. One of them appeared to be asleep, another was hiding behind a sheaf of papers but the third waved me to a chair on which I perched.

There was a short silence and then one of the interviewers emerged from behind his papers, gave me a beaming smile and said, "Ah yes, Miss Field, I see they need someone to teach Music at Bweranyangi Girls' School. I understand you sing."

I wondered if I was being interviewed for the right post! However I was willing to try anything.

"Yes," I agreed tentatively. It was hardly the time to mention that my enjoyment of singing was hardly a qualification for teaching Music!

"That's all right then," he said, obviously relieved. He shuffled some papers and then peered at me over his glasses. "Oh you'd be teaching English as well."

I was glad to hear it.

"You're not afraid of having your head cut off, are you?" suddenly barked the somnolent gentleman.

Slightly startled, I admitted that, although I wasn't very enthusiastic about the idea, I did realise the possibility of such a thing happening was not, perhaps, quite so remote in the wilds of Africa as it was in England. They nodded approvingly and, after a short conversation with each other, carried on solely by the raising and lowering of eyebrows, the first one turned back to me and announced he was sure Bweranyangi would be delighted to make use of my services. I hoped Joan, the Headmistress, would agree. It must have been the shortest interview on record, I reflected, as I floated out of the office on a pink cloud with bubbles of excitement dancing a polka inside me.

The next few months were spent unravelling myself from yards and yards of governmental red tape. I was sure some was still clinging to me as I finally stepped on the plane. I was equally sure there was bound to be something I'd overlooked which would hinder my entry into 'the Pearl of Africa'.

Fortunately my fears were groundless. Having gone to sleep over a gloomy rain-sodden England, I woke to bright sunshine glistening on a sparkling dew-washed land. As I stepped out of the plane into a bath of warm air, the heat-white buildings sizzled at me and I hurriedly burrowed into my bag for my dark glasses. Having put them on, I was able to appreciate my surroundings a little better.

Apart from their black skin, the African ladies in their rainbow costumes with puffed sleeves, bustles and parasols could have stepped straight from the pages of a nineteenth century history book. But I wasn't given time to study them. Black hands suddenly seized my luggage and hustled me through customs before dumping me unceremoniously in the arrival hall, gasping for breath.

I looked round. No one seemed the least interested in my arrival. I'd been told I'd be met by the Education Department. But after I'd been staring helplessly around for some time, a dapper African gentleman, immaculately dressed in a grey suit, accosted me.

"Mees Field?"

"Yes."

He checked his list. "Good. I look after you." Flinging out his arms, he grabbed the nearest porter who seized my cases and climbed up to the roof rack of a nearby coach while I found a window seat inside it.

Just as I was congratulating myself my troubles were over, a familiar white face swam into my ken. It was Betty, an old school friend and sister of my new Headmistress. I knew she was the bursar at Bweranyangi school but I wasn't expecting to see her at the airport. Wildly gesticulating, she motioned me out of the bus.

"What are you doing there?" she demanded when I joined her.

"The Education Department put me there."

"Joan wrote to say we'd meet you but I expect they forgot as usual."

She turned to engage my erstwhile escort in heated discussion. I tried to forget a certain reference to the 'cutting off of heads'. Butterflies fluttered in my stomach as I conjured up visions of a public execution for having offended the prevailing 'powers that were'.

At last she turned to grin at me. Clutching her in case she vanished into the nightmare of my imagination, I gabbled that I didn't want to offend my new employers.

"Oh don't worry," she said airily with the voice of one used to the intricacies of African diplomacy. "He'll only think, 'It's that Bweranyangi lot again, always whisking off their new staff before we have a chance to post them some where else'."

"Good gracious! Do they really do that?"

"Sometimes. Come on. I've got the car over there."

"What about my luggage?"

"He's getting it down."

I squinted upwards, relieved I wasn't going to lose my belongings as soon as I arrived. The porter gave me an irritated look as he clambered down and practically threw my cases at me.

The next day we drove out of a Kampala simmering in the heat and passed through the green undulating hills whose folds appeared to have been moulded by the gentle hand of a benign giant. The ochre-red soil and occasional flame tree proved a brilliant contrast to the lush green vegetation of banana groves and elephant grass. It wasn't long before we left the tarmac road and bumped along for the rest of the way on the more common red mud or 'murram'. The school was in the district of Ankole and was forty miles from Mbarara, the nearest town. So I was to fulfil my ambition to work in 'the bush'.

After several hours, we turned off the 'main' road and I had my first sight of the scattered buildings that made up Bweranyangi school. Some were wooden with corrugated iron roofs while others were whitewashed mud and wattle. We came to a stop in front of one of the buildings and I eased my cramped limbs from the car. But I soon forgot any discomfort as I absorbed the beauty surrounding me. The sun was slowly sinking into the hills making the banana plantations glint golden green against the silver white of the buildings. We were on top of the world with the horizon gracefully scalloped around us in shadowy folds of misty green. But I wasn't left to contemplate this beauty for long as it grew suddenly dark. It took me several seconds to realise this was because we'd been surrounded by dancing black figures lustily singing at the tops of their voices. My hand was seized and pumped enthusiastically up and down. I lost control of it as it was passed round the grinning circle in time to the music. I couldn't see Betty; presumably she, too, had been engulfed by the welcome committee.

I was just wondering if I'd have to spend the rest of my life at the centre of this revolving musical wheel when I glimpsed daylight and, to my relief, Joan appeared. The Africans, still singing, drifted off, waving cheerfully.

"You must be exhausted," said Joan. "Come and have some supper. Then I'm sure you're ready for an early night."

I certainly was. I'd been getting more and more tired as we travelled and even being 'sung at' by myriads of Africans, hadn't really woken me up. All I wanted to do was curl up and go to sleep.

"Do you think I'm suffering from sleeping sickness?" I said, drowsily. "I could sleep for a week."

Joan laughed. "Don't worry. You're not used to the altitude yet. We're six thousand feet above sea level here. We all go to bed a lot earlier than in England."

"Thank goodness. I really thought I must be sickening for something. I'd forgotten about the altitude. By the way what were they singing?"

"Tukutendereza. It means 'Praise the Lord'. You'll hear it wherever the Christians meet. They usually greet each other with it."

"It sounded nice but it was a bit bewildering."

"You'll get used to it. The Balokole are much more vocal in their praise than we Anglo Saxons are."

"The Balokole?"

"The born again Christians."

"Oh." I didn't like the term but I knew what she meant. "Are there many of them here?"

"All the house staff and many of the girls. The teaching staff are all committed Christians as you know. We're all English apart from Faith who's from this area. I think I told you the school used to be mission but recently the Government's taken it over."

"Yes. I know you're all missionaries and I'm the first non missionary teacher to come here."

"We're glad you're here. Unfortunately the Africans have this idea that it's only missionaries who are Christians. It will be good for them to meet you—a Christian who's not a missionary."

I remembered how, as a little girl I'd wanted to be a missionary in Africa. I never thought my dream would come true but here I was, doing the same work as all the 'real' missionaries at the school.

The next day I was shown round the campus and taken to the little house which was being built for me.

"It's got all 'mod cons'—when they work," Joan assured me. "But I'm afraid they built it the wrong way round so your housegirl has that gorgeous view from the kitchen while she's washing up and you look out on the school buildings from the living room!"

I laughed. "Why did they do that?"

"The African doesn't appreciate the beauty of nature like we do. I suppose it's round him all the time and he's used to it. Look, the second bedroom faces the view. You could use that as a study."

"Yes. I'll do that."

Rucwere, the 'headman' or caretaker of the school joined us and I went through the hand shaking routine again.

"We very happy you here, Mees Marione," he said, giving an extra syllable to my name. "We like English. You love Lord Jesus?" He sounded anxious.

"Yes I do."

"That good. All one family together." He beamed and waved as he walked off.

Joan looked after him. "He changed completely when he became a Christian," she said. "He used to beat his wife and children and get drunk. He stopped doing that and built them a better, cleaner house and treated his wife as a person instead of part of his goods and chattels."

"Is his wife a Christian?"

"Yes, she is now and so are all his children. Oh by the way there's a Fellowship Meeting on Saturday. Would you like to go?"

"What?" I'd never thought to hear that expression again.

Joan gave me an odd look. "It's where all the Balokole get together."

"Oh. What happens?" I asked curiously.

"There are hymns and prayers and readings from the Bible. Sometimes people talk about spiritual experiences they've had."

"So there's no set pattern."

"Not really." She obviously sensed my hesitation. "You don't have to come if you don't want to."

I shook off my doubts. "Of course I'll come. I'd like to."

But first I had to teach my pupils the intricacies of the English language. It wasn't long before I knew there was something wrong. But it was some time before I realised the new girls found my native English difficult to understand as they'd always been taught by Africans. They were too polite to ask me to speak more slowly and so I had to discover this for myself. Once I did, things went far more smoothly.

The Fellowship Meeting on the following Saturday was an interesting experience and for the first time I realised what a great uniter Christianity was. There were Africans from different tribes, Asians and Europeans all meeting together in love. The tribal conflict in Uganda was as great as elsewhere on the continent but here all tribal and racial differences were forgotten. We were all 'one in Christ Jesus'. I reflected that no United Nations' peace initiative could bind people together as securely as Christianity did. How I wished some of the Exclusive Brethren could experience the love that pervaded this crowded meeting.

But I cringed when the terms 'Brothers and Sisters' were used. I knew they were Scriptural but to me, 'Sister' resurrected the rigidity of the Exclusive Brethren and I didn't want to be reminded of the trauma of a few years ago.

After the Meeting I had another reminder of the Brethren that startled me. I was accosted by an elderly African whose dark eyes snapped in his wrinkled face as he barked at me, "Are you saved?"

"Y-yes," I quavered.

"When were you saved?"

"I—I—don't know."

"How do you know you're saved? Have you born fruit?"

I looked wildly round. Had I been transported back to my childhood in the Woking Meeting Room? But no. The sun was still beating down and I could see more black faces than white. He was still staring at me, waiting for an answer but my mind was paralysed just as it had been in those far off days.

"Marion, I've been looking for you." Joan hurried up. She spoke rapidly in the local dialect to my interlocutor and bore me off. "He's quite a character. Did he ask you if you were saved?"

"Yes and he wanted to know 'when'. I couldn't answer him. I felt awful."

"Don't worry. He terrified Betty the first time she met him but he's quite sweet really. The Balokole don't understand why some Europeans can't put a date to their conversions because so many of the Africans are converted so dramatically, you see."

A few weeks later I saw the result of one such conversion at first hand. Joan had told me about Kasente, a clever girl, with a great love of books which eventually led her into trouble. She came from a very poor family and books to her represented the riches she couldn't have. When opportunity came her way, she stole some from the Library. She was discovered and suspended from the school. It must have been the ultimate disgrace for her to be taken home in the middle of the term. She'd been told she would be expelled if she repeated her offence.

She'd now returned and was in one of my classes. Traces of the resentment she obviously felt were still evident and I didn't find her an easy pupil. She wasn't a Christian as many of her classmates were. But when a Mission was held in the school, Kasente was one of the girls who accepted Christ as her Saviour and recognised him as God's Son. But her conversion didn't result in the bubbling happiness evident in the other new converts. She was still deeply unhappy. I tried to talk to her after class one day.

"What's the matter, Kasente? You love Jesus now, don't you? So if you have a problem, why don't you talk to him about it? He'll help you sort it out."

She looked at me, mournful brown eyes swimming in tears. "Big problem, Madam. Me not know what to do."

"Why don't you tell me what it is? Perhaps I can help you." She shook her head. "Then tell Jesus, Kasente. He'll understand, whatever it is."

She buried her face in her hands and sobbed. I put my arms round her and prayed for her. Gradually her sobs subsided and she looked up.

"I go to Mees Hall. You come too."

"Of course I will."

"Please you wait here. I get books."

She ran off and I waited for her. Presently she returned, clutching two library books. I made no comment and she, too, was silent as we walked across to Joan's house. Kasente knocked on the study door and we entered to find her sitting at her desk.

"I think Kasente has something to tell you," I said.

Kasente brought the two books from behind her back and put them on the desk.

"I steal them again," she said, "but Jesus he tell me to bring them back and say I very sorry. Never will I steal again. Now I go to pack because this time you expel me." She turned towards the door.

Joan stood up. "Wait, Kasente." The girl turned. "Are you really sorry, Kasente? You promise not to do anything like this again."

"Oh yes, Madam. Jesus come into my life and he help me not to do bad things again."

Joan smiled. "I shan't send you away, Kasente, because I believe you. I know you won't steal again. It was brave of you to bring the books back when you thought you would be expelled."

Kasente shook her head. "Not brave. Jesus helped me."

Joan nodded. "I understand. Off you go now and do your homework."

"Yes, Madam. Thank you, Madam." She beamed and ran off. I was very moved. I'd never before seen the power of the Holy Spirit at work in such an obvious way.

I stared after her. "I wish some of the Brethren could have seen that," I mused. "I think they'd get quite a shock to see what's going on here."

"They never had any meetings in Uganda, did they?"

"No. The only Exclusive Brethren Meetings on the continent are in South Africa."

"Didn't they have missionaries?"

"No. I always wanted to be one, you know. That's why I wanted to come to Africa."

But now I wasn't sure I was the right material for a missionary. I was beginning to feel a little claustrophobic in this isolated outpost of Christianity. We went out rarely and the community, both European and African, was a very closely knit one. Prayer meetings were held frequently in Joan's house. While I felt guilty if I didn't attend, I often felt very uncomfortable when I did.

The Brethren's ruling that 'women should keep silent in the Assembly' was deeply ingrained in my being and I could no more have opened my mouth to pray during one of these meetings than I could fly. In Fellowship Meetings too, the women as well as the men took part and I was aware the Africans thought it very strange I never spoke. Joan and the other women missionaries often preached at meetings and their status was equal to that of African men. The African women usually spoke of spiritual experiences they'd had recently or 'confessed' to 'impure thoughts' or 'bad behaviour'. My English upbringing also rebelled against the idea of baring my soul in public.

I felt sad I didn't measure up to Balokole standards but there was nothing I could do about it. Soon however, I had even greater cause for concern.

Kasente came to visit me one evening after she'd been to a local Fellowship Meeting. She was in tears.

"What on earth's the matter, Kasente?" I cried, opening the door and escorting her to the nearest chair. She continued to sob while I waited for her to calm down.

At last she managed to speak. "Mr Tumuboine, he say I can't be Christian if I wear short skirt and—and—necklace." She broke into sobs again as she fingered the offending object.

I shut my eyes in disbelief. Had I misheard? But no I hadn't! History was repeating itself. Had I leapt out of the frying pan into the fire!

"And he tell Florence it wicked to let hair grow."

This bewildered me. St. Paul had forbidden women to cut their hair. They'd been instructed to let it grow. Suddenly light dawned and I had to resist an urge to giggle. An African has to cut her hair; if she doesn't, it will grow out like a bush all round her head. But I knew fashionable young ladies, like Florence, let theirs grow and then had it straightened—*à l'Européenne*. I, on the other hand, cut mine and had it curled!

So 'exclusivism' seemed to be rearing its ugly head in the Pearl of Africa and I wasn't happy. I comforted Kasente and assured her that her outward appearance made no difference to her status as a Christian. I even made her laugh by telling her I'd been told not to cut my hair and I'd often been in trouble for wearing a necklace.

But I was worried. Did all the Balokole feel the same? Did the Europeans hold the same views? As in the Brethren, man-made rules, not Scriptural ones, were being imposed and I knew from bitter experience where that could lead. How ironic it was that having left the Exclusive Brethren, I should find myself in a similar position.

For several days this dominated my thoughts but I didn't feel I could discuss it with anyone. It wasn't until Betty raised the subject one morning as we were having coffee together I realised I wasn't the only one to be concerned by what was happening.

"Did you know Tumuboine's group have broken away from the rest of the Balokole?" she queried.

"No. I hadn't heard. Why?"

"They were getting too strict. Rules and regulations—no short skirts, necklaces, ties … "

"Ties?" I interrupted, startled.

"Don't ask me why they've decided against them. Vanity, I expect."

"So they've brought in man-made rules too—just like the Brethren," I sighed.

"But at least the rest of us don't go along with them."

"Thank goodness." I breathed a heartfelt sigh of relief. "I was so afraid I'd be caught up in something similar again. I couldn't bear it. I know they don't exactly approve of me because I don't take part in meetings but … "

"Don't worry about it," advised my friend. "I don't speak either but I don't get het up about it. You've got to get rid of this burden of guilt you hump around with you. It's a sin really, you know."

"What!" I'd never considered that but now she'd mentioned it, I could see she had a point. I grinned. "OK, I'll try but it's not going to be easy. I've had it for too long!"

"Good girl. We're going to visit Katambozi on Saturday. Would you like to come?"

"Oh yes please. Where does he live?"

"In a Bahima settlement. We'll have to walk some of the way but you don't mind that, do you?"

"Of course not."

"Verinah will come with us. You remember her? We met her at the Fellowship Meeting last week. We're very privileged, you know. Most of the Europeans who come out here never get to visit any of the Africans' homes. But the Balokole all welcome us because we're Christians too."

"I've already realised how Christianity unites all races and tribes. It's not so noticeable at home, is it?"

On Saturday Betty, Verinah, a charming girl who spoke very good English, and I set off for our trip. It was pleasant to get away from the school for a little while, I thought, as I drove over the usual bumpy road trying to dodge the pot-holes.

"I don't know much about the Bahima," I said as I negotiated a particularly unpleasant one. "How do they live?"

Verinah, who belonged to the tribe, was happy to talk about her people. "They are nomadic people who own herds of cattle. They usually stay in a settlement about three months before moving on. But my family built a permanent house when we became Christian. But some Christians, like Mr Katambozi, still live in the settlement we're going to today." She broke off to peer at the road. "You turn off here."

I did so and continued to bump and crash over something that no longer bore any relation even to a footpath. "I can't go any further," I announced at last. "We'll get stuck. As it is, I'll have a job to turn round. Is it far from here?"

"Very near," said Verinah leaping out of the car. "We'll walk from here."

She set off at a brisk pace and I started to follow her, immediately falling into a camouflaged ditch. Picking my-self up, I haughtily ignored Betty's giggles and tried to find a path. There wasn't one so we waded through the under-growth trying to keep our guide in view until, to our relief, we came to a clearing. In front of us was a circle of grass huts surrounded by a wooden fence.

Suddenly we were in the middle of a colourful, cheerful crowd who swept us towards one of the larger huts and deposited us on a mat outside it. Then I looked in horror at the glass which was immediately thrust into my hand. I hated milk!

"It's smoked," said Verinah, watching me. "It's nice. Try it. They'll be offended if you don't."

I girded up my stomach to receive the unwanted beverage and took a tentative sip.

"It is nice," I said in surprise. It was sweet and the smoky flavour obscured the milky taste which always reminded me of school breaks. I actually enjoyed it.

When we'd finished, Mrs Katambozi, our hostess, disappeared into the tiny hut and reappeared clutching two black wooden pots which she thrust at Betty and me chattering animatedly. We looked helplessly at Verinah who translated.

"She wants to give you these milk pots as a gift to remember her by. She says you have done great honour to her house by visiting it and you are her sisters because she knows you love the Lord Jesus like she does."

I was deeply moved. I knew these people had so little and I was so rich by comparison and yet, because I was a Christian, she was giving me something that was of great value to her. Once again I was being taught a lesson I could never have learnt from the Exclusive Brethren.

When I returned home, I found a letter from my father waiting for me. My parents wrote regularly and like all ex-patriots, I lived for letters from home. But this one contained news that reminded me of the shadow still hovering over us.

My sister had just given birth to her third child, a little girl. Tears welled up. I hadn't even known she was pregnant. How I would have loved to buy things for my two little nieces and nephew. I loved babies and I longed to be called, 'Auntie Marion'. But there wasn't much chance of that, I thought sadly. I felt sorry for Meriel. I was sure she didn't really want to cut herself off so completely from her family. She must have felt sad at not being able to show her new baby to its grandparents.

I read on and suddenly there was a gleam of hope.

"The baby's called 'Esther Marion'," my father wrote. "So Meriel hasn't forgotten you. I was so pleased when I heard."

So was I. I rushed over to the house which Betty shared with Joan to tell them the news and we had a celebratory cup of tea.

That night I dreamt Meriel and her family withdrew from the Brethren and we were able once again to be a normal family. When I woke up, the dream was still so vivid I was sure it would happen some time.

The following Monday evening I was on duty. I was making my way in the dark towards the dormitories when I suddenly heard the most chilling, blood curdling scream. For a moment I was disorientated and then, to my horror, I realised it had come from one of the dormitories. Galvanised into action, I sprinted across and flung open the door. The room was like a scene from a horror movie. The girls, the whites of their eyes rolling in fear, were crouching on the floor, their attention riveted on Florence, who was flinging herself round on her bed, emitting the most unearthly shrieks. She seemed possessed and in that eerie gloom I almost believed she was. I discarded the possibility she was having an epileptic fit as her cries and her movements were unlike any I'd ever seen. I sent up a quick prayer for guidance and moving swiftly to her bedside, I snapped at her, "Florence, stop behaving like this. Sit up and tell me what's happened."

She ignored me, continued to scream and flung her arms out in my direction. I ducked.

"She say her brother killed in Kampala," the girl from the next bed whispered to me.

"What?" I turned towards the speaker—a silly thing to do as this time Florence's flailing limbs found their mark. I gasped. It felt like a blow from a hockey ball. I tied to pinion her arms but it was hopeless. She was much stronger than I was, particularly in her distraught state.

I glanced surreptitiously at the other girls. They were still too frightened to move. They obviously felt their companion was possessed by an evil spirit and I was beginning to feel the same. I could almost sense an evil presence. If they were right, there was only one answer, wasn't there? But life in the Exclusive Brethren had definitely not taught me how to exorcise evil spirits. I wondered how Mr Wickens would have coped.

Carefully avoiding any more blows, I edged closer and managed to place my hand gently on Florence's head. The name of 'Jesus' made the devils flee, I knew. I wasn't sure how to pray in this situation but no doubt I'd be given the right words. I was.

"Lord Jesus," I prayed aloud, "please take away the evil that is surrounding Florence at the moment. Please calm her and give her peace."

Gradually the girl's head stopped twisting, her muscles relaxed and her screams turned to a quiet sobbing which died away as she slept. I stared at her in awe. Of course I shouldn't have been surprised at the result of my heartfelt prayer but I was. I'd never before had such a sense of the tangible presence of the Lord Jesus. I knew he'd been there beside me because I couldn't have calmed the hysterical girl by myself.

"Oh thank you, Lord," I breathed as I pulled some blankets round Florence and lifted her head on to the pillow. Soft rustlings around the room told me the girls, too, had relaxed and resumed their preparations for bed.

I whispered, "Goodnight," and tiptoed out on shaking legs. Once outside, I took some deep breaths and then headed for Joan's house where I found her, grave-faced, listening to the B.B.C. World Service news. The reporter was describing street fighting in Kampala!

"Is it serious?" I asked. "Florence has just had—well some sort of fit because she thinks her brother's been killed." My flesh crawled. "How could she have known?"

"Bush telegraph, I expect," returned my headmistress laconically. "It's far more effective than radio."

She switched off. "Don't look so worried. It'll blow over. It always does and we're out of the way here. Go to bed. You look tired."

I was exhausted but found it difficult to sleep. I could still hear Florence's unearthly screams.

The trouble in Kampala lasted several weeks. We were marooned on our desert island as the only road leading out of the area had been slashed by troops. It was nothing personal, of course. We just happened to be en route to the airport!

It was rather frightening to think we were trapped but we carried on our work normally and eventually we heard the trouble was over. Apparently the Ugandan President, the Chief of the Bagandan tribe, had been ousted by Dr. Milton Obote, the Prime Minister, who'd taken over the Presidential powers.

My two years in 'the Pearl of Africa' flashed by and all too soon I was on a boat bound for my homeland again. I'd learnt a great deal while I'd been away and wondered how I'd adapt to England again. I hadn't lived there since I'd left the Brethren six years previously.

Chapter Twelve

Full Circle

It felt strange at first to be living in Woking and not going to the Meeting. But I wasn't the same person who'd left England six years previously. I'd changed both inwardly and outwardly. My hair had been cut and restyled, I wore make up and I was usually hatless when I went out! However I liked hats so I always wore one in Church.

"You look about ten years younger than you did when you were in the Meeting," my father told me appreciatively.

I laughed. "You and Mummy have shed about twenty years, too."

I'd become reconciled to my parents' membership of the Church of England and was even beginning to think my father was right about their many similarities to the Brethren. Apart from the clerical system and the set services, the basic doctrine differed not at all from what I'd been taught. They even used one cup for Communion and baptised babies, unlike some of the nonconformist Churches. And the Creed set out the beliefs of the Christian Church so clearly.

"What a pity the Brethren never used a creed," I sighed one day as we walked home from morning Service. "If they had, Mr Taylor wouldn't have been able to bulldoze people into accepting everything he said."

"I think God had his hand over it all, though," mused my father. "You don't really wish you were still bound up in that system, do you?"

"Certainly not," I said emphatically. "I'd never go back to anything like that. You were right. I like the safety net the Creed provides. After all it can't be changed without the consent of Parliament and the Queen, can it?"

"No. That's certainly one of the main advantages of being a State Church," agreed my father.

He'd blossomed since he'd joined St. Mary of Bethany. He was a sidesman, often led Bible studies and even preached at one of the special Sunday afternoon services which were held for elderly people who weren't able to attend the normal Church Services. I was amazed! He'd never taken any part in Meetings! But he obviously enjoyed his preaching and he was very good. No doubt the Dale Carnegie course he'd taken so long ago was bearing fruit.

One day he startled me. "How would you like to preach instead of me, next Sunday?" he asked.

"What?" I thought I'd misheard. Some Brethren edicts were so deeply ingrained, I found them almost impossible to reject. One of these was the silence of women in 'the Assembly'. "But I'm a woman," I objected.

"So? It was the women who remained with the Lord at the Cross and I think the missionary societies would have collapsed if it hadn't been for the women."

He was right, of course. The ratio of female missionaries to male in Uganda alone must have been about ten to four.

"But I don't think I could," I said at last. "They thought I was very odd in Uganda because I could never open my mouth in Fellowship Meetings."

"Well think about it."

I did so. It wasn't that I was any more nervous than the average person about speaking in public. I'd done so on many occasions but speaking in an 'Assembly' setting was different. Besides, my voice always quavered and I got very emotional when I talked about Christian things. On the other hand, I'd learnt a great deal in Uganda and perhaps I should share some of my lessons with a wider audience.

"What would I talk about?" I asked my father the next evening.

"I thought you might like to use some of your African experiences, linking them to a Bible reading, of course."

I could certainly do that but I still had reservations. "Wouldn't the Vicar mind me preaching?"

"Of course not. He says he'd be delighted."

"Oh." I digested this. "You're sure it would be all right. I mean, er, me being female and, er—you know …"

"I'm sure it will be all right. I think you'd make a very good preacher."

I took a deep breath. "All right. I'll do it."

He grinned and gave me a hug. "You'll be fine. I'll help you."

As it happened, I didn't need his help. Having overcome yet another hurdle I found my 'sermon' flowed and when I came to deliver it, I was able to speak without a tremor; once I'd overcome my initial nervousness, I even enjoyed it.

This led on to other talks until I felt I'd like to spend all my time speaking to groups of interested people. But it wasn't lucrative and I couldn't continue to live off my parents. It was time I found myself another job. I bought the teachers' guide book, the Times Educational Supplement, shut my eyes and stabbed my finger at the appropriate page. It landed on Ranelagh School in Bracknell which was pleading for an English teacher. I didn't want to brave the elements on the hockey pitch any more. I'd always hated the cold and after four years in centrally heated gymnasiums and two years in sunnier climes, I didn't fancy being exposed to the rigours of an English winter.

My application resulted in an invitation to meet the Headmaster who fortunately approved of me and I started work at the mixed Grammar school after Christmas. It was to prove my happiest job although at first I was very conscious of my gownless state; I had no degree and gowns were still worn in the classroom. However, my concern lessened somewhat when I overheard a sophisticated third year observe to his friend, "I do wish the staff didn't wear those things. They look like bats flying down the corridor."

This didn't, of course, diminish my pride several years later when I was one of the first Open University students to be awarded a degree and was thus able to join the other 'bats'.

During this time I started to develop my interest in Drama—even daringly directing a school play—Dickens' *A Christmas Carol*. It was a great success and I was delighted I was at last able to use this talent which God had given me. No longer did I have to 'hide my light under a bushel'.

However, when the Deaconess from my local parish Church put a proposition to me, I was startled. I'd rented a flat in the area and we were having coffee there after the morning Service when she buttonholed me.

"We're going to have a Mission in October and I thought perhaps you could produce this for us." She handed me a typewritten script. 'Alive' was stamped in bold letters across its cover. "It's the Gospel story but it's been brought up to date. We've got a guitarist who's interested in playing for the songs and we hoped some of your pupils might take part. I know you do a lot of Drama at school and *A Christmas Carol* was superb."

"Thank you," I murmured, still staring, bemused, at the pamphlet in my hand. My mind had started its familiar kaleidoscopic whirling. Producing a school play was one thing; directing a religious play to be performed in a Church was quite another. I'd come a long way since I'd left the Brethren but I wasn't sure I'd come that far! I still had strong reservations about religious drama. Surely the Brethren had been right to insist it was irreverent to portray the figure of Christ or even other Biblical figures. We never sent religious Christmas cards and although my liberal father had taken me to the national Gallery with its wealth of Old masters, some Brethren refused even to set foot in an Art Gallery because so many medieval paintings had Christian themes.

But we were living in a very visual age, I reminded myself. How many people today actually read the Bible—even in its new translations? I thought of the Middle Ages when people couldn't read. Then, too, they'd relied on the spoken word. To keep the Gospel alive the monks had dramatised the Bible stories, acting them out, first in the Churches and then eventually in the market places so the people would know what God had done for them.

Perhaps there was a similarity today when people preferred watching the serialisation of a book on television to reading the book itself. I realised June was still waiting for my answer.

"I'm sorry," I said, my mind still churning. "Do you mind if I let you know later? I'd like to look at the script first." Coward, I thought. That's not the reason you're stalling.

"Yes, of course. I didn't expect an answer straight away. Perhaps you could let me know next Sunday."

"Fine." That gave me a week to decide whether this was another 'edict' I'd discard.

"I do hope you'll do it. We need someone with a deep faith and sound Bible knowledge. You have to feel what the play is saying, not just understand it with your mind. You would do that. Think carefully about it."

"I will," I promised.

I made myself another cup of coffee and sat down to peruse 'Alive'. Brought up on a diet of the Authorised version of the Bible, the very free translation of some of the famous words grated. But it didn't change the message, I thought, staring thoughtfully out of the window.

Jesus was as real today as he'd been two thousand years ago. The people he'd healed, talked to, argued with and comforted were no different from those I met every day. They'd used the language of the time with all its modern idiom. They wouldn't have talked in a special language just because Jesus had been born. There wasn't anything sacred about any translations of the Bible, I reflected. It was the message it transmitted that was important. And what better way to show people the Gospel message than by acting it out in all its compassion, grimness and triumph?

I shut my eyes. "Please, Lord," I prayed. "Show me if it's right for me to do this. You know how difficult I've found it to go against things I was taught in the Brethren.But I know they weren't infallible so perhaps they were wrong about this too."

I didn't receive a blinding Damascus light to show me the way but when I looked at the script again, I saw immediately how it could be adapted to suit my style of direction and how it could bring the Gospel alive in the parish Church.

I didn't wait a week. I phoned June immediately. She was delighted but warned me it would be hard work. I wasn't afraid of that. The next few weeks were a frenzy of activity. I co-opted some of my pupils and church members of all ages were involved. It was the first time I'd directed adults and I was a little apprehensive about telling my elders what I wanted them to do. But they all worked well with me.

I almost drove them into the ground but they were very patient when I insisted we went over and over sections of the script until we got it right. The music was lively and I was also able to incorporate some dance movements using members of my school Dance Club.

The single performance was given on a Saturday evening at the beginning of October. The Church was packed and as I sat in the audience, I was as moved by the timeless story as they were. Jesus' words were as vivid and appropriate for a twentieth century audience as they'd been when he'd first spoken them.

During the 'Last Supper' with the Vicar's approval, the 'disciples' offered the bread and wine to all members of the congregation so they became fully involved. But the climax was an even more moving experience. The Church was plunged into darkness at the moment of Christ's death on the Cross and as I sat there in the silent Church, I could feel the tears starting to flow. Then softly from all round the building came the words, "He's alive; he's alive." Then, as the lights blazed, the voices reached a crescendo blending into the stirring sounds of Handel's *Hallelujah Chorus.*

I wasn't the only one with tears streaming down my face at the end and with this first vivid experience of dramatising the Gospel message, I was in no doubt it would be the first of many such productions I would do.

Gradually many of the attitudes and ideas with which I'd lived for much of my life were being remoulded into my new life style. I didn't regret my upbringing. I knew I'd been well taught about Christian things; constant exposure to the Bible and discussion about it meant that I knew it much better than many of my contemporaries who'd grown up in the Anglican Church. I appreciated what the Brethren had taught me although I was still sad about the break up of so many families including my own.

In the early seventies rumours about the latest eccentricities of the Brethren started to circulate among ex-Brethren. Things had deteriorated even more and ten years after I'd left, there was another exodus.

One balmy evening in May the phone rang. I picked it up, still thinking about the papers I was marking.

"Marion, it's me."

My mind blanked and I hastily sat down. I shut my eyes wondering if I was dreaming.

"Marion? Are you there?"

I was having difficulty finding my voice. My lungs weren't functioning properly and my tongue wouldn't move.

"Marion?" There was an element of panic in the familiar voice.

"Meriel?" I croaked, retrieving my voice at last. I couldn't believe it. I hadn't spoken to my sister for ten years.

"Yes. how are you?"

She sounded as normal as if we'd met the previous day.

"I'm fine. How are you?"

"I'm expecting another baby."

"Oh." I still felt rather bemused. "Er—how many's that?"

She sighed. "It'll be our fifth. We didn't really want another one but I guess the Lord overruled us."

"When's it due?" Had she really rung me just to tell me that?

"Next month."

"I hope all goes well for you," I said politely.

"Thank you." There was a pause and then she said quickly, "We've left the Brethren, Marion."

"What?" Had she really said the words I'd been waiting to hear for ten years?

"We've left the Brethren and …, and I'm sorry I haven't seen you for so long. When the baby's born, we want you to come and visit us."

"I'd love that," I said fervently, adding wistfully, "I've been longing to see the children."

"Angie's seven now. She's the oldest and Bruce, the youngest, is two."

"You must have your work cut out," I said, my imagination running riot at the thought of four children all under seven.

"It's certainly exhausting sometimes. So you'll come next month?" She sounded anxious.

"Of course I will. And you'll let me know the minute the baby's born, won't you?"

"I promise. 'Bye now."

" 'Bye."

Carefully I replaced the receiver. Then I started to shake. Suffering from shock, even a pleasant one, isn't an enjoyable experience. I staggered into the sitting room and poured myself a small brandy—kept for medicinal purposes only, of course! Then I cried, for the wasted years but, most of all, in relief that at last we could be a real family again and I had at last become an 'auntie'.

Bridget was born in the middle of June and soon after my sister returned from the hospital, I drove to the tiny farm house in Sussex where she was living. I was excited but apprehensive too. Would my suddenly acquired nieces and nephews like me? I did hope so. I dressed with care and as I climbed out of the car in front of the house, I glimpsed a small figure in the doorway. Before I could approach her, she rushed into the house, shouting, "She's wearing a midi—and lipstick!"

Oh dear, I thought. Surely I wasn't going to be in trouble already. I was wearing very little make up! I needn't have worried. Angie, my eldest niece, who'd apparently been overawed by the sudden appearance of this mysterious 'aunt', reappeared and submitted to a kiss. The door was open and I entered to find a small stocky figure standing open-mouthed in the middle of the room.

"And what's your name, darling?" I asked, stooping down to her level.

"Esther 'Auntie Marion'," a gruff little voice replied promptly.

Tears pricked at my eyes. So my sister had made sure her second daughter knew she'd been named after her 'auntie'. I hugged her and she giggled. A solemn little boy appeared in the kitchen doorway.

"This is Kenneth," Angie informed me.

"Hullo, Kenneth." As I was still on the floor, I crawled over to hug my nephew.

"Brr, brr." I jumped as some peculiar noises came from a nearby cupboard. I located it at last to discover a plump two-year-old with his hands gripped round an imaginary wheel.

"Bruce likes cars," explained my guide. "He always plays in the cupboard."

"Hullo. I didn't hear you arrive. Have you met everyone?" My sister appeared on the stairs with a bundle in her arms. I gazed at it and slowly stood up. Meriel smiled. "Have you ever held such a tiny baby before?" she asked as she gently placed my new niece in my arms.

"I don't think so. She's beautiful." I hugged the tiny bundle. Her eyes were closed and there was a soft down of fair hair on her head.

The new arrival had prevented any awkwardness there might have been between us. Meriel looked little different from when I'd last seen her. I was relieved she made no comment on my appearance. It was the first time I'd met Roger, my brother-in-law, but, like the rest of the family, he made me welcome and , to my relief, it was as if the past ten years had been obliterated.

The following year the family moved from Sussex to Taunton to a larger farmhouse and my parents and I were invited for Christmas.

"It's the first time we've celebrated Christmas properly with the children," my sister told me shyly, soon after we arrived. "They've never had a Christmas tree and I wanted them to have one this year. Will you help me choose one?"

"Of course." It was cold so we were wrapped up in woolly hats and scarves as we drove into Taunton.

But she'd left it too late. We searched and searched but all the Christmas trees had gone. I could sense my sister's disappointment and knew this meant more to her than just a tree. It had become a symbol. I said one of my quick prayers. "Please Lord, you know how much this means to her. Please help us find a tree."

We'd bought some decorations for it but we still had no tree as we sadly started to drive home.

"Look!" I suddenly grabbed Meriel's arm causing her to swerve. "Stop. Look. There are some trees in that garage."

There were six magnificent trees from which to make our choice. My sister beamed. "Oh, I'm so glad you saw them."

"It wasn't really me. I did say a quick prayer."

We all had great fun decorating it although fifteen month old Bridget was more of a hindrance than a help. She obviously felt the pretty silver balls were there exclusively for her benefit and, as soon as we put them on, she tried to pull them off.

It was the best Christmas we'd had for years as we were all together again. Sadly, it was the last one we were to have together as the following April my father died peacefully in his sleep.

My mother refused to phone my sister or me until the following morning and she stayed alone in the house despite the doctor's protests.

"I know where my husband is," she told him, "and the same Lord who's taken him, will take care of me. I don't want either of my daughters driving through the night to be with me."

It was a sad time. I'd always been very close to my father and I missed him greatly. But how glad we were that Meriel had been reunited with him and he'd been able to enjoy a Christmas with his grandchildren. He and my mother had moved to a village in Hampshire only ten months before he died and the funeral service was held in the Parish Church he'd been attending. The Vicar from St. Mary of Bethany came from Woking to officiate and my father was laid to rest in the churchyard.

My mother coped amazingly well. She was popular in the village and had already made many friends. She was happy too in the Parish Church. Meanwhile, on the strength of my Open University degree, I was appointed Head of English at a school, which to my amusement, was near Woking. I found a house there and thus returned to my roots.

Next door lived a young couple with two small children. I was rather startled when I recognised the husband as Paul Harrison. He'd been a small boy in the Woking Meeting when I'd left the Brethren! I knew he was still 'in' the Meeting so I wasn't surprised therefore at his embarrassment when he discovered his new neighbour was the original 'scarlet woman'! My view that God had a sense of humour was reinforced by the house he'd chosen for me!

It was in a block of four town houses and therefore joined to that of the Harrisons and so I waited for developments. I knew the latest decree was that Brethren weren't allowed to live in houses attached to any owned by 'worldly' neighbours. I, of course, was even worse as I'd known 'the Light' and turned my back on it.

I'd recently heard of a case where a brother had actually applied for planning permission to create a fifteen inch gap between his house and that of his neighbour 'on religious grounds'. I wasn't surprised the application had been turned down with the comment from one counsellor that it was the most ridiculous reason he'd ever heard.

I wondered if a similar application would be received from Paul but he obviously decided discretion was the better part of valour and the family decamped, moving to the other end of the town.

The Parish Church of St. Paul's was just round the corner from my new house so I went there on the Sunday after I'd moved. I found it warm and welcoming and I felt I'd at last found my spiritual home. Soon I was teaching the Pathfinders, directing and acting in Drama sketches and even becoming Secretary of the Parochial Church Council. I'd come a long way since my Brethren days!

But the shadow of the Brethren still hovered and before long I was jolted into vivid memory by a traumatic event within the Church, triggered by a statement from the Vicar at the Annual Church Meeting. As Secretary, I was next to David when he gave his report. Pencil poised over the paper, I gradually stopped writing as I couldn't believe what I was hearing. Although there had been indications that David wasn't completely happy with some of the doctrine of the Church of England, I'd thought naively his problems had been ironed out by the Bishop and the Church Wardens.

They hadn't apparently. To my horror, we heard an authoritarian statement describing the direction in which David was determined St. Paul's Church should go. Unfortunately, much of what he was saying was contrary to Church of England doctrine, including his refusal to baptise infants. He was speaking against the vows he'd made at his ordination and there was no doubt he was sowing seeds of discord. He would only stay as Vicar on his terms, he told us, and if we couldn't accept them, he would leave and take like-minded members of the congregation with him.

"And members of the Parochial Church Council who don't agree with my vision," he ended, "must resign."

I'd given up any attempt to take notes. I felt sick, my legs were shaking and tears were pouring down my face. I'd been this way before. I remembered with horrid clarity the Care Meeting at which Mr Hutton had been 'withdrawn from'. I couldn't face the same situation again.

But then the voice of reason intervened. "Don't be absurd," it hissed at me. "This is the Church of England, not the Exclusive Brethren. David's on his own. No one can change the rules of the Anglican Church without reference to the General Synod, Parliament and the Queen. Remember this is the State Church—not a tiny minority group."

I recovered sufficiently to hear the cultured voice of Clive, one of the Church Wardens, reinforcing my thoughts.

"The Vicar is showing a lack of love for the flock he has promised to lead faithfully. He's said he doesn't feel he can baptise babies which is one of the responsibilities of a Church of England vicar. If he feels he can no longer keep the vows he made in the presence of God and this congregation, the problem is not ours but his." He looked directly at David and said gently, "If you feel you can no longer fulfil your obligations, you have no alternative but to give your resignation to the Bishop."

David was not impressed. "If God wishes me to lead this Church in the vision he has given me, I shall stay—on my terms," he insisted.

By now, I was not the only one who was sobbing. David was obviously not going to give way and was convinced he was right. How well I remembered a similar intransigence!

Then Clive spoke quietly again. "I don't think this is either the time or the place for this issue to be discussed. I move we bring the meeting to a close."

I couldn't get out of the hall quickly enough. I was still crying and scattering papers all over the floor as I left. I didn't want to go though another traumatic division! I couldn't face it!

"You won't have to," urged the voice of reason again. "This is the Anglican Church not the Brethren."

The next day I finished school at the start of the Easter holidays which I was spending with my mother. I was relieved to be going away from Woking and its reminders of what had happened nearly thirty years ago.

Early the following morning, the phone rang. It was Clive. "I know how upset you were on Tuesday evening," he said gently, "so I wanted to let you know David has seen the Bishop who has persuaded him to resign."

"Oh thank goodness," I gasped. "I was so worried."

"I know you were." Then he added the words I'd been saying to myself. "But this is the Church of England, you know, not the Brethren."

"I realised that but it still came as such a shock."

"Well he's gone and now we have to pray for the right man to take his place. The Bishop is coming to the eight o'clock service on Easter Sunday. Without a Vicar, we wouldn't be able to have a Communion Service."

"Oh, how thoughtful of him!" I exclaimed.

"He's very concerned about his flock here and has promised to help in any way he can."

So I could enjoy my holiday without worrying and when I returned, I was pleased to discover no one had left the Church to follow David. The congregation was still intact.

But the experience had made me think. I'd appreciated the safety net provided by the creeds and the thirty nine articles of the Church of England and for a while it had seemed this was about to be slashed from under me. For the first time I started to consider Confirmation. Perhaps it was right, after all that I should become a full member of the Anglican Church. For some time I'd been happy to take Communion but hadn't felt it right to be confirmed as I'd thought that was for new converts to Christianity.

But now I reread the Confirmation Service and realised I should, of course, be confirming my faith—something I was quite happy to do. I obviously hadn't read it properly before.

It was two years later that I finally approached Steve, our new Vicar, to say I should like to be confirmed. He'd recently announced he was starting some Confirmation classes and that had given me the nudge I needed. I'd already told him about my background.

"I don't think you need to attend the classes," he said with a grin. "How about coming round to the Vicarage one evening and we'll have a chat. Oh by the way you have been baptised, haven't you?"

"Oh yes, when I was a baby."

"That's all right then."

I enjoyed our talk tremendously and we ranged over a vast number of topics—the Second Coming, the rebuilding of the Temple, the Millennium. I found it stimulating and became more and more convinced the basic doctrine of the Church of England didn't differ at all from the Brethren. Admittedly in both groups there were people who followed their own line but while Mr Taylor had been able to force the Brethren to follow him, no one in the Anglican Church had any power to do the same thing. This had been conclusively illustrated by the recent disturbance in St. Paul's Church.

A few weeks before the Confirmation Service, I made a decision and approached the Vicar after the morning Service.

"Steve, I'd like to explain to the congregation why I'm being confirmed. I'm sure some of them will be surprised to know I haven't already been—er—done. Not many people know about my background. Could I speak during the service next Sunday?"

"Of course you can."

He was always willing for members of the congregation to share experiences in the Services. Our form of worship was very much freer than I'd originally expected in an Anglican Church. We were certainly not rigidly bound by the Prayer Books and only some 'set' prayers were used.

It was the week before the Confirmation Service that I spoke. It was the first time I'd given a public testimony in Church and I was very nervous. I also wanted to make sure I said exactly what I wanted to say. Therefore, although by now, I had no trouble speaking in public, I decided to read my statement so I could think very carefully about it beforehand. I didn't want to upset anyone or say something controversial.

This was the final result of my deliberations:

" I want to tell you why I'm going to be confirmed and why I haven't taken this step before. Many years ago it would have been customary for only those who'd been confirmed into the Church of England to take Communion in an Anglican Church. But for some years now, many Churches, including this one, have prefaced their Communion Service by inviting all those who love the Lord to participate in the Lord's Supper. On that basis I have done so for many years.

"The reason I haven't been confirmed before is because I felt I'd already taken a similar step when I first asked to remember the Lord at his Table as a member of the Exclusive Brethren Fellowship in my teens.

"I was brought up in that loving fellowship which was firmly grounded in the Scriptures and although the services were informal and there was no Prayer Book to follow, the Creed that we say every week sets out clearly the basic tenets of the Christian faith to which the Brethren adhered so closely.

"Sadly in the nineteen sixties the Exclusive Brethren movement started to disintegrate as some of the leaders moved away from the Scriptures and, with many others, I left. At that time, although my own faith wasn't affected, I felt a sense of insecurity because I no longer belonged to a closely knit fellowship.

"But all my life I've been a citizen of the Kingdom of God and for the past few years I've worshipped with other citizens of that Kingdom in this Church.

"I now wish to strengthen my earthly security by becoming a full member of that part of God's Kingdom on earth, the Anglican Church, and so it seems right that I now take the step of being confirmed."

The Confirmation Service was the following Sunday evening. I was delighted my sister agreed to come but sad my father wasn't there to share the day with me. Although he, himself, had never been confirmed, I felt he would have approved—as my mother did.

There was a tea before the Service and I was introduced to the Bishop. "I'm so sorry we don't have a Service to welcome someone like you into the Church," he said, smiling. "But I shall have great pleasure in confirming you into the Church of England."

"Thank you very much." I was warmed by his words. "It's taken me some time to come to this decision but I'm sure it's the right one."

It was a moving service and in his sermon the Bishop reminded us that our bodies were the temple of the Holy

Spirit and should therefore be respected. The love of God, he said, was like a triangle with God at the apex and his people in the centre. His love came down to us and ours should ascend to him.

As he placed his hands on my head, tears were very near the surface. I felt I'd come full circle. I'd returned to that very same Anglican Church from which Mr Darby and others had withdrawn themselves over a century before. I had a feeling that if they were here today, they, too, would return to the fold.

A Window To Heaven

Dr Diane M. Komp

What would you do as a hospital doctor when children facing death—or their parents—witness to you about faith? The official line is not to get involved, to stay 'professional'. But that was not Dr Komp's reaction …

'I have met people who claim they lost their faith over the agonising question, How can a loving God let innocent children die? Dr Komp is the first person I've met who found a personal faith while treating such dying children. Her story —and theirs— deserves our attention'.
Philip Yancey
Author of *Disappointment with God*

'Unforgettably inspiring'
Sandy Millar, Holy Trinity Brompton

'Out of harrowing experiences while looking after children with cancer, Diane Komp, a paediatric oncologist of international repute, draws conclusions about the human condition that should make us pause and think …
I read it with a lump in my throat.'
J.S. Malpas D.Phil., FRCP, FRCR, FFPM
St Bartholomew's Hospital, London
ISBN 1-897913-32-X
Highland Books   Price £3.99

Shut Up Sarah
by
Marion Field

Was she privileged? Sarah was born into the Taylorites, the most exclusive of those Brethren who look to J N Darby as founder. You may have seen them:

- Women with scarves who stick together
- Schoolchildren who never accept invitations
- Groups of men declaiming the Bible on the street

This true story of a teenage daughter refusing to be browbeaten by either family or elders will be compulsive reading for mature teenagers struggling between loyalty and the need of change—as well as for any who want to understand how certain Brethren could have lost their way.

'I highly recommend this book ... This gifted writer in her second book has written a true story in a compelling fictional style.'
Jennifer Rees-Larcombe

ISBN 1-897913-28-1

Highland Books   Price £5.99